A LIFE WITH ANTIQUE CLOCKS

Derek Roberts

4880 Lower Valley Road Atglen, Pennsylvania 19310

Other Schiffer Books by Derek Roberts:
Precision Pendulum Clocks: The Quest for Accurate Timekeeping. ISBN:0-7643-1636-2. $79.95
English Precision Pendulum Clocks. ISBN:0-7643-1846-2. $99.95
Precision Pendulum Clocks: France, Germany, America, and Recent Advancements. ISBN:0-7643-2021-1. $99.95
Mystery, Novelty & Fantasy Clocks. 0-7643-0873-4. $150.00
British Longcase Clocks. ISBN:0-88740-230-5. $95.00
Carriage and Other Traveling Clocks. ISBN:0-88740-454-5. $99.95
Continental and American Skeleton Clocks. ISBN:0-88740-182-1. $79.95

Cover designed by: Bruce Waters
Type set in Adobe Jenson Pro

ISBN: 978-0-7643-3378-1
Printed in China

Schiffer Books are available at special discounts for bulk purchases for sales promotions or premiums. Special editions, including personalized covers, corporate imprints, and excerpts can be created in large quantities for special needs. For more information contact the publisher:

Published by Schiffer Publishing Ltd.
4880 Lower Valley Road
Atglen, PA 19310
Phone: (610) 593-1777; Fax: (610) 593-2002
E-mail: Info@schifferbooks.com

For the largest selection of fine reference books on this and related subjects, please visit our web site at **www.schifferbooks.com**
We are always looking for people to write books on new and related subjects. If you have an idea for a book please contact us at the above address.

This book may be purchased from the publisher.
Include $5.00 for shipping.
Please try your bookstore first.
You may write for a free catalog.

In Europe, Schiffer books are distributed by
Bushwood Books
6 Marksbury Ave.
Kew Gardens
Surrey TW9 4JF England
Phone: 44 (0) 20 8392 8585; Fax: 44 (0) 20 8392 9876
E-mail: info@bushwoodbooks.co.uk
Website: www.bushwoodbooks.co.uk

Contents

Acknowledgements

My first acknowledgement must be to my wife Valerie, whose help and tolerance has made my journey through the world of antiques, and in particular the writing of so many books, possible, involving as it has such a large number of hours shut away in the study and also a lot of travelling.

My second acknowledgement is to all the staff of Derek Roberts Antiques who have supported me so ably and fully in all my endeavours. In particular I should mention Rosemary Freeman, who has typed out most of my manuscripts, some of which, before the age of computer technology, had to be produced more than once. In the latter period Elizabeth Stracey also gave much help in this respect. Following the passing of my business to Paul Archard I lost the services of these two ladies, but was fortunate enough to find a worthy successor in Julie Francis, who has produced the manuscript for this book for me, with some technical assistance from her husband Peter.

John Martin, with whom I have worked closely for many years, has made a major contribution to this book, in part because of his partnership with me in constructing some 38 regulators and assisting in their documentation, but also in researching and restoring several of the complex clocks that have passed through our hands, of which the most fascinating example is the clock by Edward Cockey, which is thought to have been the one made by him for Queen Anne. I am also most grateful to him for proof-reading this book.

Throughout the time I have been involved in the world of horology, which is now over 40 years, I have received advice, support and, above all, information from a large number of people. One of the first was Ronald Lee, sadly no longer with us, who approved my membership of The British Antique Dealers' Association. He had an extensive library and a fine collection of photographs and was always ready to share his knowledge with others, as was Peter Gwyn, his partner at one stage. Another was Charles Allix, who wrote, after much research, the first book on carriage clocks. Since then there have been many more, including museum staff, auction house personnel, research workers, collectors and dealers.

Other authors have also been most helpful. Hans Staeger, supplied and allowed me to reproduce much information and material from his book, *100 Years of Precision Timekeepers from John Arnold to Arnold and Frodsham, 1763-1862*. Dieter Riefler permitted me to reproduce extracts from his book on Sigmund Riefler, and Hans-Jochen Kimmer and Herbert Dittrich gave me permission to use material from their book on Strasser and Rohde.

The craftsmen I have worked with, who had a wide variety of skills, have also been a superb font of knowledge, both in demonstrating, often so apparently effortlessly, their skills and in analysing and passing on helpful comments about the clocks that passed through their hands.

Alison Young, of H M Revenue and Customs, gave me information on the Value Added Tax (VAT), from its introduction in 1974 until 1997, and Mr. P J Martin, Inspector of Taxes, answered all my queries on Interest and Inflation Rates, Recessions and exemptions from Capital Gains Tax. I am most grateful to a friend, Mr. K Ladd, for carrying out much statistical research for me at the Institute of Directors. Catherine Scantlebury and Carolyn Moore of Christies kindly gave me details of the Buyers Premium, from its inception in 1975 until June 2008.

It is the summation of information from all these people, and indeed many other sources, that has enabled me to write my books and thus permitted me to pass that knowledge on to others.

Introduction

This book, which is really my swan-song, tries to trace a dealer and author's career in horology from its beginning in the 1960s to the present time. It illustrates the mistakes that can be made so easily and the achievements realized as well as some of the more amusing and unusual incidents that have occurred along the way.

It starts in the early days when there were far more dealers and large quantities of virtually all antiques available, be it furniture, clocks, porcelain, glass, etc. Today antiques, particularly those of fine quality, are hard to find and strongly competed for.

The book covers the effect of the introduction of VAT, which added greatly to the paperwork involved in running an antiques business, and at a later period the Buyers Premium, which dramatically increased the cost of buying at auction. Comment is also made on the three recessions, all different, which were encountered and the ways they were dealt with.

It is hoped that the book will appeal not just to dealers and auctioneers, but also to collectors to help them understand "the other side of the fence" and the way in which serious dealers can help them in acquiring, adding to and refining their collections. They can also advise on items coming onto the market, which might be of interest, and assist with valuations and insurance.

Chapter 1
Before Clocks

When I reached 18 we were still in the era of National Service, which was of two years duration, but I was given deferment from this to allow me to qualify in dentistry, provided I was accepted for and started dental school within four months.

This was something of a difficulty as, for no particular reason, I had idled my way through school. There had been no problem with the School Certificate, taken around fifteen to sixteen, but the Higher School Certificate, which one sat two years later, had been a different matter, requiring far more dedication. The upshot was that I was short of credits in one foreign language and physics if I was to be accepted at the school where my father and sister had studied before me, the Royal Dental Hospital. This meant, in effect, that I had to resit these two exams in mid-December, just three months away. It was then, for the first time in my life, that I started taking studying seriously.

The help of a particularly forceful lady, Miss Hotchkiss, who had retired some years ago from the local girls school where she taught French and had always been respected, was enlisted for this subject.

To gain a pass in physics, I attended a 'crammer' called Borlands where a Mr Burfitt, if I remember correctly, taught physics with great enthusiasm and in a way which was easily understood. One of the things I still recall about him was that he always wore an immaculate blue suit but unfortunately had the habit of leaning against the blackboard which was covered with his writings in chalk and was disastrous for his clothing and, to a lesser extent, his calculations.

December came and, to my relief, I succeeded in getting the necessary credits in both exams and started at the Dental School in January. The previous three months proved to be invaluable as they taught me the pleasure to be gained from the acquisition of knowledge, something which has never left me.

Having qualified rather more than four years later, in November 1952, I duly went into the RAF after having been granted a one month extension to my deferral because I had been given an entry in the Monte Carlo Rally. It was a pleasant time when I like to think I made some contribution to the dental services, checking over, for instance, the personnel due to go out for the atomic tests in Australia, when even then the complications of radiation were beginning to be appreciated. Pay was by no means high, I started at £12 a month and

finished at £28, but I learned to glide and fly, went up from time-to-time in the Canberras operating on our station and even did quite a bit of horse riding, the local farmer charging me only two shillings and six pence for the 2-3 hours I generally went out for. He was just glad to get his horses exercised. On occasions, it cost me a little more as I would stop at one of the pubs for a pint, and one particular horse expected some beer too and if he didn't get any kicked up quite a fuss.

The few years in the forces gave me time to think, and whilst I realised I had a good basic knowledge of dentistry, I wanted to know more. To this end I did start some studying, but realised that the only way to acquire a greater depth of understanding of the subject was to do the Fellowship Course, the first year of which was at the Royal College of Surgeons, the fount of so much knowledge and where many of the lecturers were leaders in their fields.

I could not afford to do this immediately after I left the forces, so applied for a place starting some six to seven months later. This gave me a chance to stock up the financial coffers so that I could, in effect, take a year off. During this year, I also earned some money in the evenings and at weekends, but I had to limit this as the course was quite demanding, sometimes taking me into areas which had not even been published in the books. Knowing that the percentage pass mark was then only around 20% was also strongly motivating.

At the end of the year, to my delight, I passed the Primary or first part of the exam for my Fellowship. To pass the final was very much a practical as well as a theoretical exam and thus it was necessary to work and study within a hospital, and the one designated to do this was the Institute of Dental Surgery, Eastman Dental, situated in Gray's Inn Road. This had the added attraction that it had a large number of attractive young nurses and it was there that I met my wife, the prettiest of them all! There was nearly a set-back at the beginning as when I first asked her out she said she thought I was married. Luckily she believed me when I said that neither was I married nor even had any children. Once again I had an interval of about six months to sort out my finances before I could start at the hospital and worked on some evenings and Saturdays.

It was here that I met up with dental colleagues from many different countries and acquired a much wider appreciation of the subject. We also had the chance to meet many of the leaders in our field. At the end of the course, having gained my fellowship in 1959, I was asked to stay on as a part-time member of staff, which suited me admirably. I gradually got involved in the teaching and was invited to investigate the design of the bridges that had been fitted, ie the holding of replacement teeth in place by fixing them to those on either side.

This proved to be a major task going through all the patient's records over many years to find those for whom bridges had been fitted and then contacting them and asking them to come in so that we could check them. If this failed, then we would write to the referring dentist asking if the patient had moved and if he had encountered the bridge recently and if so let us have a condition report.

Gradually, with the help of further letters and phone calls, we had traced around 75% of those patients who had had bridges fitted and felt that it was unlikely that the remaining 25%, most of whom had moved away, would have any appreciable effect on our statistics.

Whilst we were carrying out this research we also instituted an annual check-up of all bridges we had fitted, which was beneficial to the patient as we could identify problems before they resulted in failures and also because it enabled us to show students a large number of different types of bridge.

The upshot of the research, which in some instances surprised us, was that we changed the design of some of our bridges, which produced a marked rise in the success rate. A full analysis of the results was published in two parts in the British Dental Journal and in due course I wrote my first book, devoted to bridge design (Fixed Bridge Prostheses), which was published in 1973.

This research had taken many years to reach its conclusion, and prior to and at the same time as this I had been collaborating with a colleague, Dr John (subsequently professor) Sowray, who was in charge of oral surgery at King's College Hospital. He had taken a different path to me because of his interest in this area, for which it was really desirable to be both medically and dentally qualified. He also subsequently obtained his Fellowship.

Dental health at that time was, particularly in certain areas, poor, and one of the main problems associated with this was people's fear of dentistry, engendered in part because many did not attend regularly and when they did do so, were in pain, sometimes severe, and could be difficult to treat.

The other reason was that the main method of preventing pain during treatment was the injection of a local anaesthetic solution. This could be administered painlessly, but to do so required a careful and delicate technique. It also had to be placed accurately, otherwise it might not work. It was for these reasons, which were reinforced by the fact that we could both remember having had painful injections during our younger days, that we decided to write a text-book on the subject.

We were fortunate in that, when necessary, we could draw on the resources of both our hospitals, although this was naturally kept to a minimum. We had the services of an excellent medical illustrator, Jennifer Middleton, and someone who could assist with the close-up photography. We also managed to find colleagues who volunteered to have the various techniques demonstrated on them; however, these were carefully contrived so that, although they illustrated the procedure correctly, no needle ever entered the tissues.

One of the more amusing incidents concerned mouth-to-mouth resuscitation. A Junior House Surgeon offered to be the guinea-pig who needed reviving and remarkably rapidly one of the nurses offered to demonstrate the technique. Unfortunately, her enthusiasm was such that we had to get them to repeat the procedure several times before we managed to obtain the pictures needed to illustrate the technique correctly. It turned out afterwards that she had been trying to attract the subject's attention for at least two months and certainly had no intention of missing the opportunity.

This was to be the most successful book I was ever associated with. It was first published in 1970, ran to three editions with 10,000 copies of the English version being sold. It was also translated into Japanese, Italian and Spanish, the latter version selling widely in South America. From an author's point of view, it is a little unnerving to look at a book which you have written but cannot read.

At the time of writing, royalties, albeit on a fairly small scale, are still coming in from South America, which is somewhat worrying as by now the book, although on its third edition, is seriously out of date, even if the same basic principles still apply.

One of the most complimentary letters came from a doctor who was the sole source of both medical and dental treatment for all those living on a small island in the Indian Ocean where a ship only called every three months. Before he left he bought a large selection of handbooks but said that ours had proved the most valuable.

Chapter 2
The Early Days

Looking back, the very casual way in which we digressed into the world of antiques continues to surprise us; however, it must be remembered that at that time stock was far more freely available and the number of dealers actively trading much higher.

We had been living in a pleasant little close in Dulwich on the outskirts of London for some seven or eight years, which had cost me the princely sum of £3,100, plus £150 for the garage, and a further £150 for the premier site looking out onto the central gardens. I still have the mortgage broker's calculations somewhere written on the back of an old envelope where he had worked out that the repayments on the endowment insurance needed to cover the full sum to be loaned, together with the benefit of 'with profits', would be just £5 a week.

Figures 1a, b. **Our first showrooms,** where we also lived above and behind, at 24 Shipbourne Road, Tonbridge, Kent. The front window was used by the ARP as a lookout post during the last war. (Above and next page)

While we had enjoyed living in Dulwich, and indeed it was where I had been brought up, we spent much of our spare time drifting out into the countryside of Kent and Surrey, and felt that we might as well live there. Thus, when Valerie saw an advertisement in the Evening Standard for a white weather-boarded 17th century cottage in Tonbridge in Kent, Figure 1a, we immediately decided to go and see it. The owner, who had bought the property some three years before, was a highly skilled cabinet maker. He had a workshop in the garden and had also created an attractive showroom on the ground floor. The cottage, on three floors, had been extended at the back to give one additional bedroom and had planning permission for further enlargement. The only problem was that he was one of those people who never finish anything. The upshot was that we agreed to buy the property provided he guaranteed to complete all the unfinished work. Sadly, plenty of promises were forthcoming but very little action, and thus when we finally moved in, much remained to be done.

The removal day was in July 1968 and happened to be the hottest day of the year. I felt particularly sorry for the two students in the removal van who were just hoping to pick up a little extra money for their holidays. The main problem, apart from the difficult passageways, was the steep flights of narrow stairs, with a right-hand turn at the top and virtually no landing. To get the double bed I had made, with drawers below to maximise space, up to the top floor, I had to literally saw it in two and then reassemble it in the bedroom.

The passing remark of the leader of the removal team "I can't imagine why you wanted to leave a lovely home for this dump" nearly reduced my wife to tears, particularly as she realised that the only storage facilities in the kitchen was a collection of cardboard boxes.

By about 11 o'clock that night we had reduced the house to some sort of order and thus feeling thoroughly hot, sticky and dirty, I decided to have a bath. I had filled it rather generously and when I got in, the water level rose well above the overflow. This did not worry me at first until I suspected that the water running away was not going down the overflow pipe. I leapt out of the bath and went downstairs to the hall which was immediately below the bathroom, only to see water flooding through the ceiling, so I dashed upstairs again and pulled out the plug. On removing the side panel of the bath it was clear that no overflow pipe had ever been installed. By the time we had cleaned up the water it was after 1 o'clock before we got to bed. This was the first of a multitude of similar ordeals which occurred during our first month.

The most important project was to make and install fitted cupboards, etc, in the kitchen and when this had been achieved, some 3-4 weeks later, we started to settle down to some degree of normality.

It was around this time that we decided to divide off the kitchen from what became the dining room. A most attractive pair of glazed doors from a Georgian bookcase or china cabinet found in the garden provided the perfect answer. They were exactly the width required and all we had to do, after restoring them, was to fill in below with some shelving on one side and a recess for flowers on the other. It was surprising at that time just how much furniture, some of it decorated with particularly attractive veneers, was being scrapped and the remains of many such items had been left around, both in the workshop and outside.

The interior of the cottage was particularly attractive and had many interesting features, such as the standard of a small decorative cast iron street lamp having been installed to support the staircase. Thus relatively little work was needed, mostly paint and filler, to complete its transformation to a very pleasant home.

The showroom on the ground floor, Figure 1b, needed virtually no attention. Our predecessor was of an artistic temperament and decorated it most attractively, putting an arch in to break it up and, at the same time, adding extra wall space.

Having dealt with the house, it was now the turn of the garden. The property had at one time been a butcher's where they did their own slaughtering, and thus there had been numerous outbuildings which had subsequently been demolished, but not removed; their contents lying all over the garden. It took some 27 full size skips to clear all the rubbish. One would be delivered between 7 and 8 in the morning, and by 12-1 o'clock it would be full to overflowing. At that time they cost £2. 15. 0. to £3. 0. 0. and we usually managed to deal with 2-3 a week. Probably the most spectacular event occurred when I put a pickaxe into a wasps nest. We had to evacuate very quickly and shut all the windows.

It was now that the pleasant part of restoring the garden started. There was the remains of an immensely strong air-raid shelter there which, even when I attacked it with the heaviest sledgehammer available, proved quite immovable. We thus gave up the attempt and built a decorative fish and lily pond on top of it, which proved a great success. All that remained was to put up a decent fence to one side, terrace the garden and lay down some ornamental paths and steps, and the foundation of the garden was born.

Initially, a few moderately small trees were planted and then the beds created, and in a short while we had a very pleasant garden which was not overlooked, and indeed from the upstairs windows we could see across to the River Medway, maybe a mile away.

We inherited some stock from our predecessor, mostly Georgian furniture, but the showroom looked somewhat colourless and uninviting, and so we started on the track of acquiring stock. Indeed, we had already bought quite a few items by the time we moved in, including three longcase clocks.

The purchase had not gone smoothly at the completion stage and this, in the end, proved to be to our advantage. We were buying the house on an endowment insurance, as with our first one, and for technical reasons, which I cannot recall now, the money could not come through from the insurance company until some 10 days after completion. I approached the bank and asked them if they would provide a loan to cover the intervening period, and on receiving a suitable guarantee from the insurance company they agreed and indeed the Bank Manager confirmed this in writing.

Having had a particularly hectic few weeks, we decided to take a long weekend away and came back a couple of days after completion, ready for the onerous task of moving. Unfortunately, on arriving home, we learned that the bank had refused to honour my cheque. Evidently the Manager had also gone away for a long weekend and had not left his assistant any specific instructions regarding the arrangements, although, of course, if he had taken the trouble to review the paperwork, he would have realised that all was in order. The upshot was that the transaction was completed a day late, with the solicitor, a good friend, putting up the money.

As soon as I returned, I went to see the Bank Manager who apologised profusely, agreed to write suitable letters to all concerned and then asked if there was anything he could do by way of recompense. I explained that I was starting up a small business in Tonbridge and could do with some working capital. I suggested a figure of £3,000 and this, to my surprise, was immediately granted without any mention of a security.

The sum of £3,000 would now only buy one mediocre longcase clock or a fairly good carriage clock; however, in 1968 a good fully restored mahogany longcase with moon phases would sell for £50; a London mahogany longcase clock fetched around £80; a marquetry clock dating from 1685-1700 fetched £150 to £200, and a simple carriage clock £8-£12. Thus for £3,000 plus the £2,000 we had, we could put on a really good display. A further factor was that interest rates were low at that time and the value of antiques in general was beginning to rise.

When we started, although the emphasis was on clocks, we also stocked good furniture and decorative items. It was at this early period also that we purchased two of the finest walnut bureaus I have ever seen. Both had beautifully fitted interiors with secret drawers and a slide. The best, which was of a marvellous pale honey colour and had a superb sunburst veneer to the fall, I offered to a friend for £300, but at the time he could not afford it and has regretted it ever since. It finally went to a dealer, who specialised in walnut furniture, for his own home.

The ease with which one could acquire stock at this period is illustrated by the copper and brass we bought to liven up the showroom. Most of it came from a lady in one of the Medway towns who, for many years, had been buying it in locally and always had it piled up, as it came in, in two or three rooms. With £100 in my pocket I could completely fill the estate-ised back of a Morris Minor. Then came the hard task of entering it all in the books, polishing and pricing it. Within a month, most of it would have sold and we were off to the Medway again. Candlesticks fetched £1. 10. 0 to £2. 10. 0; coal scuttles £6-£8, and good early measures maybe £3-£10. I remember buying a full set from 4 gallons down, some eight in all, for £45.

So far as longcases are concerned, the simple but good oak 30 hour, preferably at that time with a single hand as these were earlier, could be bought for about £10-£12 and after overhauling the movement, restoring the dial and attending to the case, fetched about £30 delivered, roughly the same price as an oak painted dial 8-day longcase clock.

Interestingly, and illustrating the lack of specialised knowledge at this period, in our first year of trading we were offered three good mahogany longcase regulators (master clocks keeping very accurate time) by general dealers who all said they couldn't sell them because they didn't strike.

There was a relatively long time between agreeing a price for 24 Shipbourne Road and completion, and during this period we visited a large number of antique dealers and had some very fruitful discussions on stock, the trade and dealing in general. A lot of the dealers we went to at that time no longer exist, and there are now virtually no large dealers who keep the very wide range of good quality antiques then available. There were several converted mills, for instance, that we visited, which kept a massive stock of furniture, both restored and un-restored, ranging from the 17th to the 19th centuries. I remember one that prided itself on always having a set of 36 Georgian dining chairs in stock with a table to match.

One of the most interesting showrooms we visited was in North London. It had started off occupying one large three-storey Victorian house and had spread into those on either side, with communicating doors at all levels. The range of goods stocked was impressive, from furniture covering the 17th to 19th centuries, porcelain, silver, clocks and many other items including a vast array of paintings, maybe one or two thousand, occupying several rooms. Only a relatively small number were hung, with the rest piled up in rows on the floor. In one room, for instance, they were all around £250, in another £500 and a third £700-800, which was a very substantial sum in those days.

My host was a genial character and seemed happy to give what helpful advice he could to a couple of newcomers. Interestingly, his main point was that you should always try to buy the best and most original example of any item you were seeking, and not be unduly influenced by price. One of the pieces he suggested to us was a ladies' mid-19th century workbox in immaculate order and with every single ivory item it started life with still in place. We sold it on the first day we opened for business.

What surprised me, being new to the trade, was the three 'runners' who arrived with laden vans whilst we were there. In each instance he bought maybe 70 to 80% of the contents of the vehicle.

'Runners' were, at that time, an integral part of the antiques world. They would scour the auctions and also the stock in many of the dealers throughout the country to try and find items for the dealers they supplied who had premises and were mainly retailers or sold to overseas dealers. They worked on quite small margins and seldom restored anything. Nowadays the shortage of stock, coupled with the advent of magazines such as Antiques Trade Gazette and the internet, where anyone can search and find out what is coming up for sale, usually all over the world, makes their survival almost untenable; however, a few do still exist, driving vast miles to try to cover everything that is coming up for sale, and on occasions representing dealers by viewing items and then bidding for them at auction to avoid their having to travel long distances. One such runner I know in this country used to regularly drive over 75,000 miles a year, whilst another on the continent, nicknamed Mr. Kilometre, covered over 125,000 kilometres. He was quite likely to be attending a sale in Holland on one day and a few days later be in Rome!

Another quite important part of the antique world in those days was the courier. These were largely employed by the shippers who used them to take round their overseas customers. The best of them had a wide knowledge of the antiques world and could take their visitors to the shops which were most likely to stock the items they were interested in and then arrange for the collection and payment. Sometimes you would be paid by the shippers, who generally gave you a cheque when the goods were collected and subsequently provided certificates of export, which became particularly important once VAT was introduced.

When we commenced trading on a small scale, we kept a record of everything we sold and our initial aim was to always sell at least one item each week. In the very early days, this proved something of a challenge. One week all we managed to dispose of was a rather unusual Victorian egg boiler. On another occasion, we had reached 2 o'clock on a Saturday afternoon without a sale when a lady walked in looking for a desk, of which we had two. She said she would have to check the space available in the room next week before making a decision; however, with our first 'duck' in danger of coming up, I offered to bring them both over to her office to see and by 4:30 pm, with one hour to go, we had concluded a deal.

Within six months sales had improved dramatically, in large measure due to our increased stock, but also because we had learned what was in demand, and an ever-increasing number of customers had found us.

It was around this time that I was told an amusing story by a clock collector. After the war there was 'demob' (demobilisation) money which you received when you left the forces, and with the help of this he became determined to buy a good longcase clock.

On the journey by bus every day he passed an antique dealer who used to lean his longcase clocks up against the front of the shop. It was something I had also seen. One day as the bus was passing, he saw a small and attractive marquetry longcase in the line and immediately rushed down, got off the bus and walked back to the shop. The clock was just what he was looking for, the price (£40) seemed reasonable, and he said he would like to buy it. He proffered a cheque which the owner declined, saying he only dealt in cash, so he asked if he could leave a deposit of £5 and pay the rest in a day or two. Unfortunately this was also declined, so he resumed his journey to work, withdrew the £40 from the bank in his lunch hour, and dashed into the shop the next morning, only to find, to his anguish, that the clock had been sold.

It was to be only a month or two later that he saw another earlier marquetry clock for sale as the bus went by. Again he leapt off the bus, dashed back to the shop and found to his delight that the clock, although an extra £5, was even better than the other one, being of month-duration and by a more prestigious maker. Again he said he would like to buy it and again the dealer said he only dealt in cash; however, this time he was ready, having carried £50 in cash in his pocket since the last incident. He collected it that night on his way home, holding it on the platform at the back of the bus (quite a feat, particularly with the two heavy weights). Bus conductors were much more relaxed and friendly in those days. Indeed, it would not now be possible.

An interesting example of the importance of stocking the best of any particular item was well illustrated by the three corner cupboards we had in at the same time. The first was a good flat- fronted oak cupboard with panelled doors, priced at £35; the next was a well figured bow-fronted George III mahogany cupboard of a good colour and patinatation that we were asking £65 for, and the third was a particularly fine inlaid mahogany corner cupboard with astragal and other glazing, priced at £95; with good porcelain in it, it looked superb. This was the first to sell in a matter of days, the second was the bow-fronted one, and some six months later the oak.

Tunbridge Ware (wooden household items on which floral and other designs, such as buildings, are created from tiny squares of wood, known as end-grain mosaic) greatly interested us, in part due to its being a local product but also because we were fascinated by the subject matter and the techniques and skill involved in its manufacture. It also made the shop more attractive and interesting to come into, and introduced something at the lower end of the price range, as by then we were already specialising in clocks of ever-increasing value.

A good way of learning, apart from books, lectures and museums, is to exhibit at antique fairs, particularly those that are vetted, as you then benefit from any criticism of your stock and by talking to other dealers. A good example of this happened with a bureau bookcase I had, which had spent its life in a big old farmhouse in Ireland where they relied on peat fires. Because of the fires, the entire bureau bookcase was covered by a thick dark brown, almost-black deposit, which took many hours of hard work to remove without destroying the original finish. On the sales tag I had given a date of origin of 1775, but the design of the upper part of the bookcase, as I should have known, correctly put the date at around 1800, and thus indicated that the two parts were a "marriage." It was only when I moved the piece away from the wall so that the entire back of the two parts could be seen to be by the same hand, and acknowledged that I had dated it 25 years too early, that the vetting committee agreed that all was well. Most fairs were usually held at the principal hotels within a 40-or-so-mile radius, and some of the fellow exhibitors of that time we still know to this day.

Many of the dealers specialised in different areas of expertise, and thus by chatting with them you could broaden your knowledge and get to know from whom it would be best to seek advice or refer a customer if the item in question was outside your field.

An example of the importance of acquiring a good depth of knowledge of a particular subject came to me early on. A dealer who specialised in books and prints, buying and selling from his home, asked me if I would like to sell some good Victorian paintings for him and I agreed, as I thought it would make the showroom more interesting. However, after about a week I thought again about the matter and realised that if I sold the paintings, I would, although I knew little about them, be guaranteeing their authenticity and thus felt I should get an expert opinion. Two of the pictures were signed by Myles Birket Foster and two by William Callow. Therefore, I phoned a good friend of mine in the art world and asked his advice. He explained that he could not give an opinion, as he seldom handled anything dating after 1700, but referred me to a colleague who specialised in Victorian paintings, and he agreed to

see me. At that time he had something like 12 to 15 paintings by Birket Foster in his stock.

He took me down to his basement where most of the paintings were hung and pointed out details on the Birket Foster paintings (such as a girl's fingers and nails and a water butt), and then compared them with the two pictures I had brought. Immediately it was obvious that mine were not of the same quality nor by the same hand.

On my return to Tonbridge, I phoned the person who had given me the pictures on sale or return and explained that I felt I was a little out of my depth in handling them and he duly took them back. I didn't entirely give up on paintings; I particularly liked winter scenes, mostly Dutch and some seascapes, but only acquired them from leading dealers in whom I had every confidence. However, as their value rapidly rose, I gave up even this limited amount of dealing.

Figure 2. **The central part of the showroom** which, in effect, consisted of three inter-connecting rooms, circa 1972.

Figure 3. **The main or front portion of the showrooms,** excluding the right hand side, together with a glimpse of the central & rear sections.

By around 1975 the showrooms were much as seen in figures 2 and 3, consisting in effect of three rooms. Originally the front showroom only had a ceiling height of about 7' 0", but we managed to increase this to over 7' 9" by lowering the floor, which meant that we could accommodate some of the taller longcase clocks that I found so attractive.

Paris

In our very early days a wealthy French doctor, who had just bought an apartment in Paris, visited us with a view to buying furniture for it. I cannot recall now all the items he bought, but amongst them was a very fine drum table and a beautifully figured George III mahogany quarter chiming longcase clock; however, one of the conditions of the sale was that we should deliver them to Paris. There was far too much to fit into our estate car and so a friend kindly offered us his quite large van which was fully fitted out, with side ties etc, for transporting antiques.

The day duly arrived and we started loading everything into the van early to give us the maximum time to reach Paris. We drove down to Dover without more ado and went onto the ferry. It was then, for the first time, that it occurred to us that we should have declared the goods when we entered France (this does not apply today), but by then it was too late and in any case we did not have the correct documentation. As we drove off the ship and through customs, we expected to be stopped at any time, but fortunately this did not happen, although for the next 10 to 20 miles we were constantly looking in the rear-view mirror for police cars.

We arrived in Paris in the early evening and by the time we had unloaded and set up the clock, it was approaching 9 o'clock. The customers wanted to show their appreciation and so took us out to one of the best restaurants in Paris. From there we went on a sight-seeing tour of the city and the lights, and around maybe 12 o'clock were at his club prior to visiting some of the night-life. By the time we had done this it must have been approaching 2-3 o'clock and as we had been up since 5.00 am the previous day, were having some difficulty, despite the scintillating company and surroundings, staying awake and were more than a little glad when we were dropped off at our hotel. The next day we could relax a little and spend some time in Paris prior to catching the evening ferry back to Dover.

The Development of the Business

At the start of the business, although we had a good range of clocks, we also stocked furniture, Tunbridge Ware, prints and maps, mostly of Kent and the surrounding area. We also dealt in prints of local buildings and had some decorative items such as copper and brass.

Valerie also dealt in jewellery and small items of silver such as vases and writing card cases on her own account, all of which were very popular and for which we had a steady source of supply; however, following a couple of thefts, maybe five years after we started, the insurance company refused to cover us unless we had two people always in attendance in the showroom and all display cabinets were kept locked. We could not comply with these two stipulations and so reluctantly Valerie gave up dealing in silver.

We enjoyed handling and restoring Tunbridge Ware and even at one stage contemplated writing a book on the subject;

however, the introduction of VAT and the large amount of paperwork it generated made dealing in this impractical, bearing in mind the relatively small profit which was made on each item and thus we ceased selling it.

Furniture more gradually fell out of the scene and even up to the time we sold the business, we still had a few good items in stock.

In the early days we liked to have a wide range of fully restored clocks covering a broad price band so that anyone, within reason, could come in and buy a clock from us for their home; however, once again, practical financial considerations became a stronger and stronger factor. It often cost no more to buy (excluding the purchase price), restore, sell, deliver and provide an insurance valuation for a clock selling for £30,000 than it does for one selling for say £3,000, but obviously the profit will be far greater and also the clock will be much better value for money. If one sells a clock for £30,000 and the cost of restoration is say £1,000, ie 3% of its value then this is relatively insignificant, but if you spent £1,000 on a clock that you have only paid £2,000 for, then this is 50% of the total cost.

The result of this was that whereas in the early years we were selling around 700-750 clocks a year, although our turnover continually increased, the number of clocks we sold steadily fell, which of course involved us in less and less work.

The Oak Dresser

During our early days, although clocks rapidly became our main business, we carried quite an extensive range of furniture, including early oak and good Georgian and mahogany furniture, and at the time in question, had sold a relatively large and particularly good quality dresser base which was due to be shipped to Germany.

The carriers arranged to collect it one evening and their van duly arrived about 6 o'clock. The driver apologised but said that as his travelling companion was off sick would I kindly help him get the dresser into the van.

I was amazed at how heavy it was but with a bit of a struggle we got it into the van; a thick blanket was put over it and it was strapped to one side. The driver gave me a receipt and went on his way.

About an hour later when we sat down to dinner I mentioned to Valerie that they had collected the dresser base, to which her immediate response was: "did you remove our pianolo rolls?", numbering around 100, which immediately explained why the dresser was so surprisingly heavy. Frantic phone calls ensued and we finally tracked the shipment down to a London dockside a couple of hours before it was due to be loaded. The next day I retrieved the rolls and all was well.

Adding an Extension

Some two to three years after we moved in, we decided to go ahead with the extension for which outline planning permission had already been granted. This was to prove far more difficult than envisaged for a variety of reasons; for instance the architect had drawn the ridge of the roof as a straight line and had omitted to take into account the fact that the land rose by over two feet from front to back, which would have resulted in bedrooms with a ceiling height of around five feet.

Eventually, after considerable negotiations, the much revised plans, which included bay windows for the lounge and main bedroom, were approved and we sought estimates from local builders. The one we selected had been doing work on a local school, which seemed a reasonable recommendation and, in due course, he started. The main specification, which we were most grateful for, was that we would not break through into the original building until it was virtually finished. This was possible because the extension was, in effect, an independent building with a garage, workshops, garden room and toilet on the ground floor, a large lounge on the first floor and two bedrooms and a bathroom on the second floor.

Within six months of starting work, our choice of builder had proved to be a very bad one. The foundations, after difficulties with the inspectors, had been laid and the walls had risen maybe two feet. Unfortunately the site was a tight one going virtually out to our boundary on either side and as no rubble etc had been removed, was so cluttered up that virtually no further building work was possible. It was at this stage that I started checking levels and found that the three outside walls were all of very different heights, although apparently one course of bricks ran around them.

I had been making stage payments, possibly a mistake as after his last payment we had not seen nor heard of the builder for some six weeks. We had a meeting and decided that we should part.

The first step was to clear up the site and as I had become quite good at filling skips by then, this was achieved in two to three weeks. Unfortunately it was a boom time, with builders much in demand and we found it difficult to find one to take on the job and it was then that a customer who specialised in small developments of maybe ten to fifteen luxury houses, stepped into the breech, offering to help in an advisory and also a practical capacity. Most of the existing walls were demolished, true levels established and a local brickie and his mate taken on at a daily rate.

Unfortunately the building boom taking place at the time had resulted in a severe shortage of bricks and we had to resort to using French ones which, although reasonable in colour, were a slightly different size.

I only got involved in the bricklaying in one or two places which were difficult to get at where the two buildings met;

however, in conjunction with my customer and friend Edward Watkinson, we laid the floors, clad the roofing, and did several other jobs, including the decorating. Finding the time to do this when I was trying to run a business and going to London two days a week meant that I was often working on the building late into the night. One of the more hair-raising experiences was transporting the completed heavy hardwood open-tread staircase from my friend's house, some twelve miles away, back to Tonbridge. It took six of us to lift it onto the roof rack of the Morris Minor Traveller. Even a slight camber in the road made me think that the car would tip over; however, all went well and the staircase fitted perfectly.

When completed, the extension gave us much pleasure, figure 4, with the large bay windows at the back giving us views over open countryside to the River Medway. An essential was, of course, the installation of an outside clock.

Figure 4. **The extension to the rear**, which more than doubled the size of the property. Note the inclusion of an outside clock!

Chapter 3
Kent Clock Services

Within a year or two of moving to Tonbridge and starting our business, the property next to us, which at that time was a chemists, with accommodation above, came up for sale.

Brian Kuwertz, who lived four to five miles away and did much of our clockmaking for us, was keen to start a business there and so it was decided that he would acquire the flat above the premises and that we should jointly buy the ground floor, which was quite commodious and he would run a repair business from there, which became known as Kent Clock Services (figure 5).

The demand for clock repairs was strong and before too long, six to seven clockmakers were busily employed. The difficulty was that with a large number of clocks going in and out, each one different and requiring different work, the business had to be meticulously run and everything carefully costed. Unfortunately, this proved difficult and within a few years the firm's finances were in a perilous state. By then, Brian Kuwertz had sold the flat and bought a house elsewhere.

To clear the finances, Brian and his brother suggested they should take over the business and the property be sold to a friend of theirs who would then lease it back to them and this is what happened.

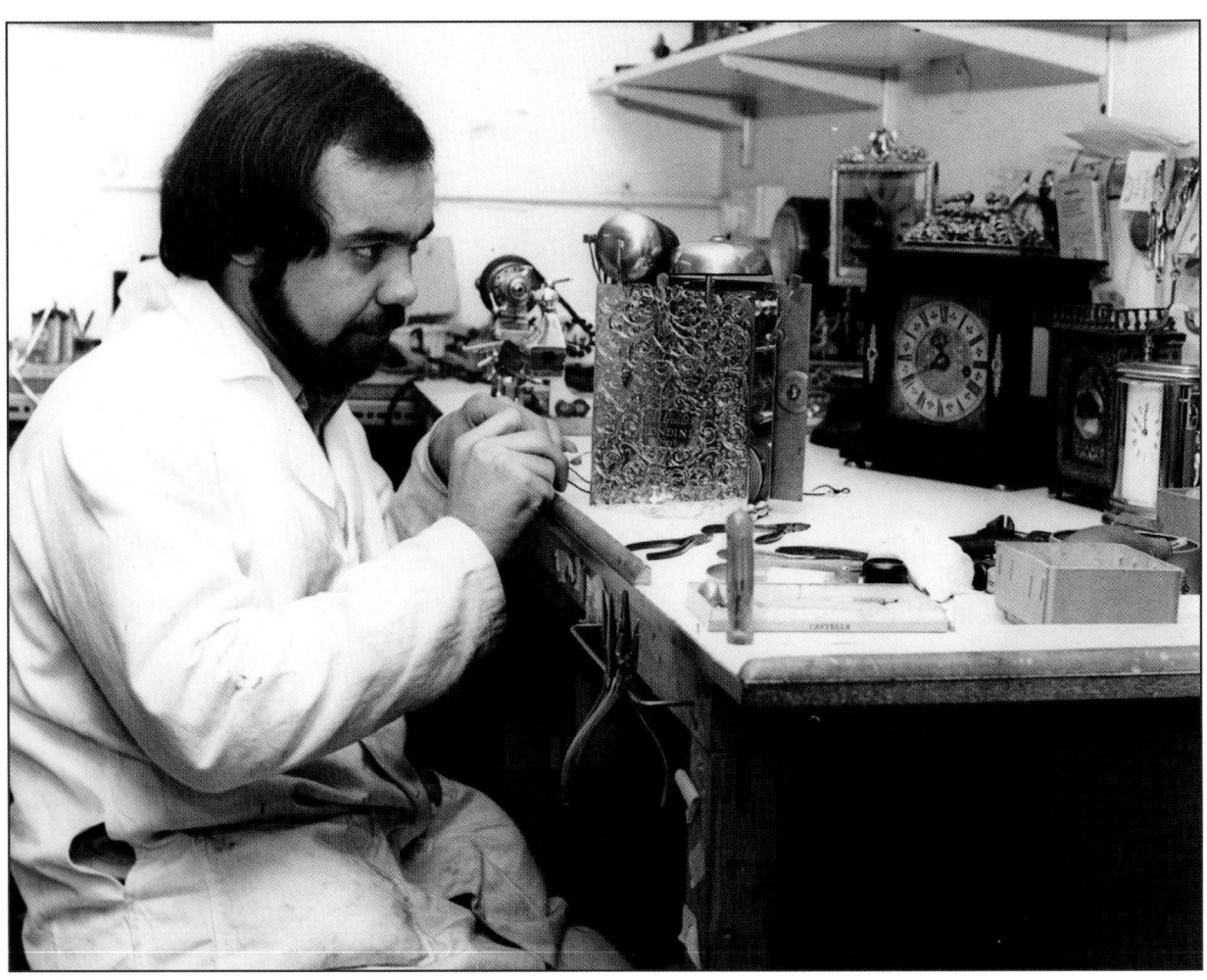

Figure 5. **Brian Kuwertz** working on a variety of clocks at Kent Clock Services.

Figure 6. **The showrooms at 25 Shipbourne Road.** The extension on the right was put on by the previous owner, a chemist.

Sadly within a relatively short time the business failed again and we then bought the premises (figure 6), which were far more suitable as a showroom than the one we had at that time; there was a much larger room and far more (10 ft) ceiling height. In the cottage we were limited to about 7' 9", even after lowering the floor, which precluded many fine but tall clocks.

I took over four of the clockmakers, who could be accommodated in a separate building and in the basement which had previously been damp-proofed and air conditioned, and Brian Kuwertz employed the rest in a converted squash court attached to his new home.

In the event, two of the clockmakers I took on left to become self-employed and the other two, with one additional member, were still with us when we sold the business.

Chapter 4
Martin & Roberts

1976 — 1999

A Brief History of the Partnership

It was in 1974 that we acquired a small Scottish regulator movement with an 8" engraved and silvered dial. Over the following two years a search was made for a suitable case, but to no avail, and thus it was decided to make one, probably not a sound commercial proposition but, as the regulator was for ourselves, this was not a consideration.

The basic parameters for the design were that it should be a wall regulator, as compact as was practical, with a seconds beating mercurial pendulum and extensively glazed to show it off. The initial design, which evolved over several months, was very loosely based on the Viennese wall clocks with glazing to the front and sides of the trunk, but employing a conventional slide off hood with glass to either side, and an architectural top.

The detailed design was subsequently worked out in conjunction with the cabinet makers E R Truphet of Borough Green, who produced the case veneered in rosewood. John Martin restored the movement and designed and made a miniaturised mercurial pendulum for it.

All those who saw the completed wall regulator were most enthusiastic, probably in large measure because of its proportions and relatively small size. This was something that was not generally available in an English antique regulator. Several people asked if one could be produced for them, which immediately introduced a problem in that, although the cases could be made relatively easily, no further existing regulator movements were available. It was in 1976 that the partnership was formed with John Martin designing and making the mechanical elements of the clocks and the first six were completed over the period September 1976 to September 1978.

The concept, right from the beginning, was to produce the best possible regulators, and thus it was decided that the pallets and pivot holes for the pallet and escapement wheel arbors should all be jewelled, and endstones employed throughout the train. The eight inch round dials were engraved and silvered, with centre sweep hour, minute and seconds hands, rather than the layout normally used in English regulators, to give them more general appeal.

Figure 7. **The first of the wall regulators produced by Martin & Roberts.** It had an eight day fully jewelled (pallets, endstones & pivot holes) movement and was available in walnut, mahogany, rosewood or satinwood.

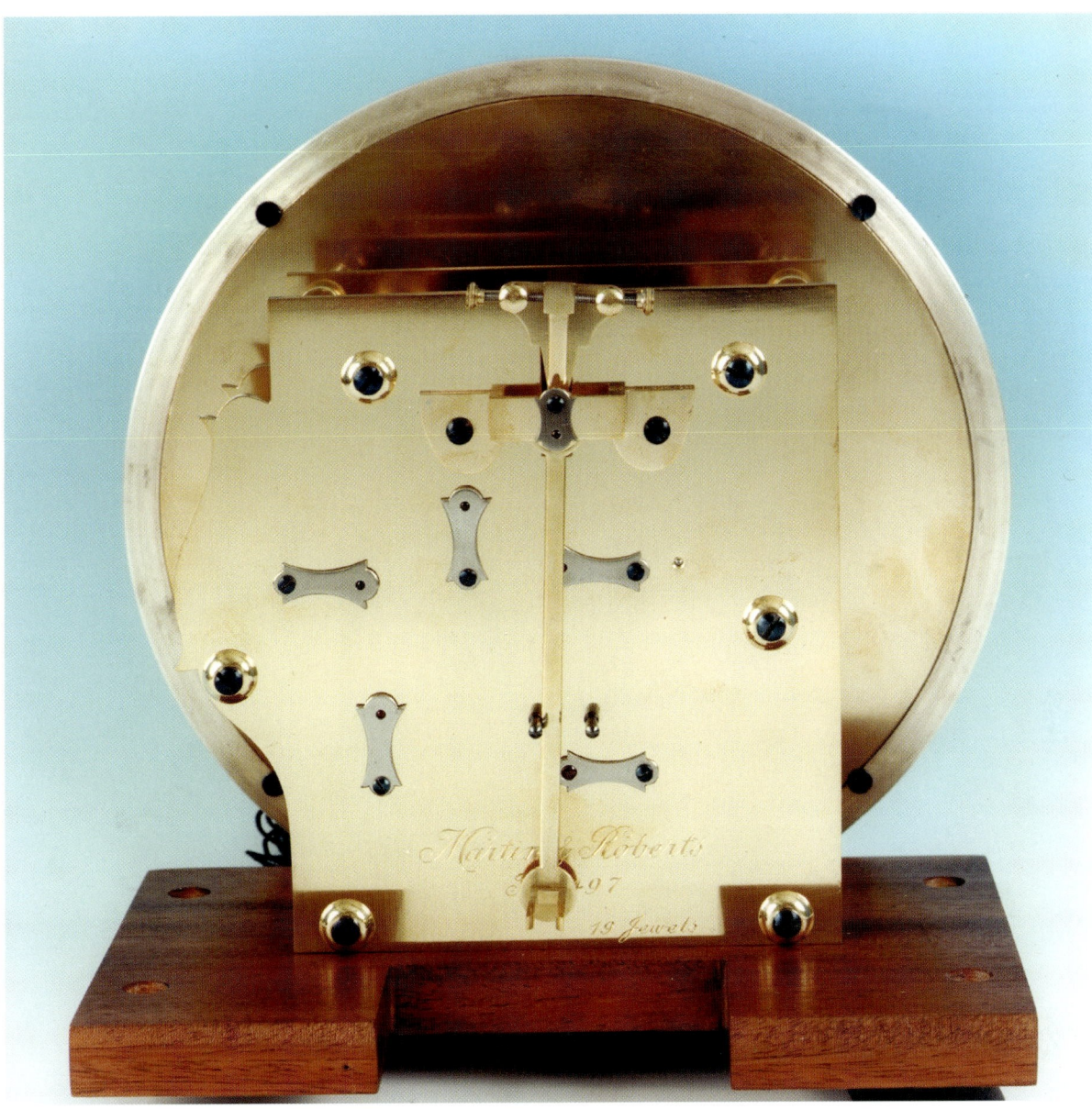

Figure 8. **The month-duration movement.** Note the extension to one side to protect the extra wheel required and the shaped steel plates carrying the jewels which act as endstones.

So far as possible, customers were offered a choice of mahogany, rosewood (figure 7), walnut or satinwood veneers. All the early clocks were of eight days duration, but subsequently several requests were received for month duration regulators and, indeed, these were to become the design requested by most customers. Because of the delicacy of the case it was felt necessary to keep the driving weight of the month clocks only a little larger than that required for those of eight days duration. Thus, not only did the number of wheels and pinions in the train have to be increased, but the whole movement had to be refined and a smaller and more delicate escape wheel and pallets employed. Additionally, the plates were enlarged and re-shaped to ensure that the wheels were fully embraced within the movement (figure 8).

It was in 1978 that it was decided to add a multi-dial clock with full calendar-work and moon phases to the range (figure 9), and initially a pair were made for the partners, one having a satinwood veneered case and the other walnut. This latter clock, No 475 was used for experimental purposes, and any subsequent mechanical changes were proved in it.

In addition to these two a further ten round dial clocks, mostly of eight days duration, were produced between 1978-1981. The first commissioned multi-dial clock, No 490, was made in 1982 for Asprey & Company, Bond Street, whose clock department was, at that time, run by Jack Pierce.

From 1981 onwards only one further eight day clock was made and this was No 489, built in 1985. This was displayed in our showrooms until the partnership was dissolved in 1999.

Figure 9. **The perpetual calendar clock** with subsidiary dials for the day (dial rotates), date, month and moon phases. Like all the other clocks, it has a centre sweep seconds hand. The case is veneered in satinwood with inlaid panels.

In 1985 it was decided to design a perpetual calendar mechanism for the multi-dial clock (figure 10). This proved a complicated project as the dial layout had been established without the possibility of change. Had the perpetual calendar concept been envisaged initially the layout would have been radically different.

The first clock to this design was No 491, made in 1984 for an American client, and encountered problems with the mechanism for leap years. Modifications were carried out on the 'experimental clock' No 475, the fault corrected and clock 491 duly modified.

From then onwards, any further clocks of the multi-dial type were built to this specification. In addition other improvements in the movements were incorporated (figure 11), such as double click-work and a spring-loaded double idle wheel to remove the backlash inherent in the minute train when a centre-sweep seconds hand is used.

Up until this point no accurate records of the time taken in the production of the regulators had been made. A client, who

Figure 10. **The under-dial work of the perpetual calendar clock.** The wheel to the right corrects for the leap years.

had had a pair of shotguns made by the famous firm of Purdy, was told by them that one thousand hours had been spent on their production. He was, therefore, interested in knowing the total time taken to make his month duration perpetual calendar clock. The figure arrived at was one thousand seven hundred hours and this was, if anything, an underestimate.

It was in the 1980s that we acquired, for our own collection, a Viennese year duration movement with wood rod pendulum having a massive fully engraved and gilded bob, but no dial. We decided to have a convex, jewelled and hard enamelled dial made to which a centre sweep annual calendar was added. This proved by no means easy but in the end a dial was made and gold paillons were produced for the decoration and jewelling. These and the numerals were added by Michael Glover, the well known dial restorer. An entirely new case design was then created to compliment the enamelled dial and extremely large fully engraved and gilded pendulum bob.

The movement needed considerable modification, in part to provide an annual calendar, but also to give the year duration with a relatively small drop. A complex system of pulleys was thus devised which a) allowed the weight to be wound up behind the movement for maximum fall and b) permit the weight to drop vertically next to the backboard.

A fully glazed case was designed with curved glass sides and a full width removable door. Because of the shape a hinged one was not practical. The clock was veneered in rosewood with satinwood stringing and a hatch added at the top to give access to the movement. The rectangular weight was engraved by Peter Fox to match the existing engraving on the pendulum bob. The case for this clock was one of the last to be made for the partnership by E R Truphet. Subsequently all the cases were produced either by Colin Buckwell, our principal cabinet maker, or Nicholas Martin (son of John Martin) of Whale & Martin, Cabinet Makers.

Figure 11. **The movement of the perpetual calendar clock.**

The year clock was duly installed in our home where it ran faultlessly for many years. There was no intention to produce any further similar clocks, in large measure because of the complexity of making such a movement and case and in particular the dial. However, in 1991, a friend finally persuaded Martin & Roberts to make one, which was numbered 496 (figure 12a).

This was a project that took some three years to complete, one of the greatest problems being to produce the 10" convex jewelled enamel dial. This was finally completed, at the second attempt, with the help of Derek Pratt, by Michel Vermot in Switzerland after the first dial was irreparably spoiled at the final glaze.

Figure 12a. **The year-duration wall regulator.**

The movement for this clock was substantially re-designed from the relatively basic Viennese movement of the first one. Many of the refinements developed by Martin & Roberts were incorporated, such as journal jewelling virtually throughout; sub plates to simplify access to the very delicate escapement; full micrometer adjustment of the pallet arbor and double click-work (figure 12b).

Because of the manufacture of this clock by Martin & Roberts it was decided that what in effect became the prototype, the one owned by us, should be signed by Martin & Roberts and given a serial number, although this would be chronologically out of order.

Approaches were made to Martin & Roberts to produce further year clocks. These were declined, in part because of the work involved and the difficulty of manufacturing the dial, and also because by this time both partners had passed their retirement age and no longer wished to take on such a long term project.

Requests were made that the clock be made under licence in the USA but this was declined on the basis that the partners would have no control over the quality of the clocks produced to their design, which had taken much time and effort to devise.

Over the entire production period from 1976-1999 some 38 regulators were made to a variety of specifications, from eight day to month and year duration, with or without perpetual calendar-work.

A schedule recording all the regulators produced by Martin & Roberts is reproduced on the accompanying sheets.

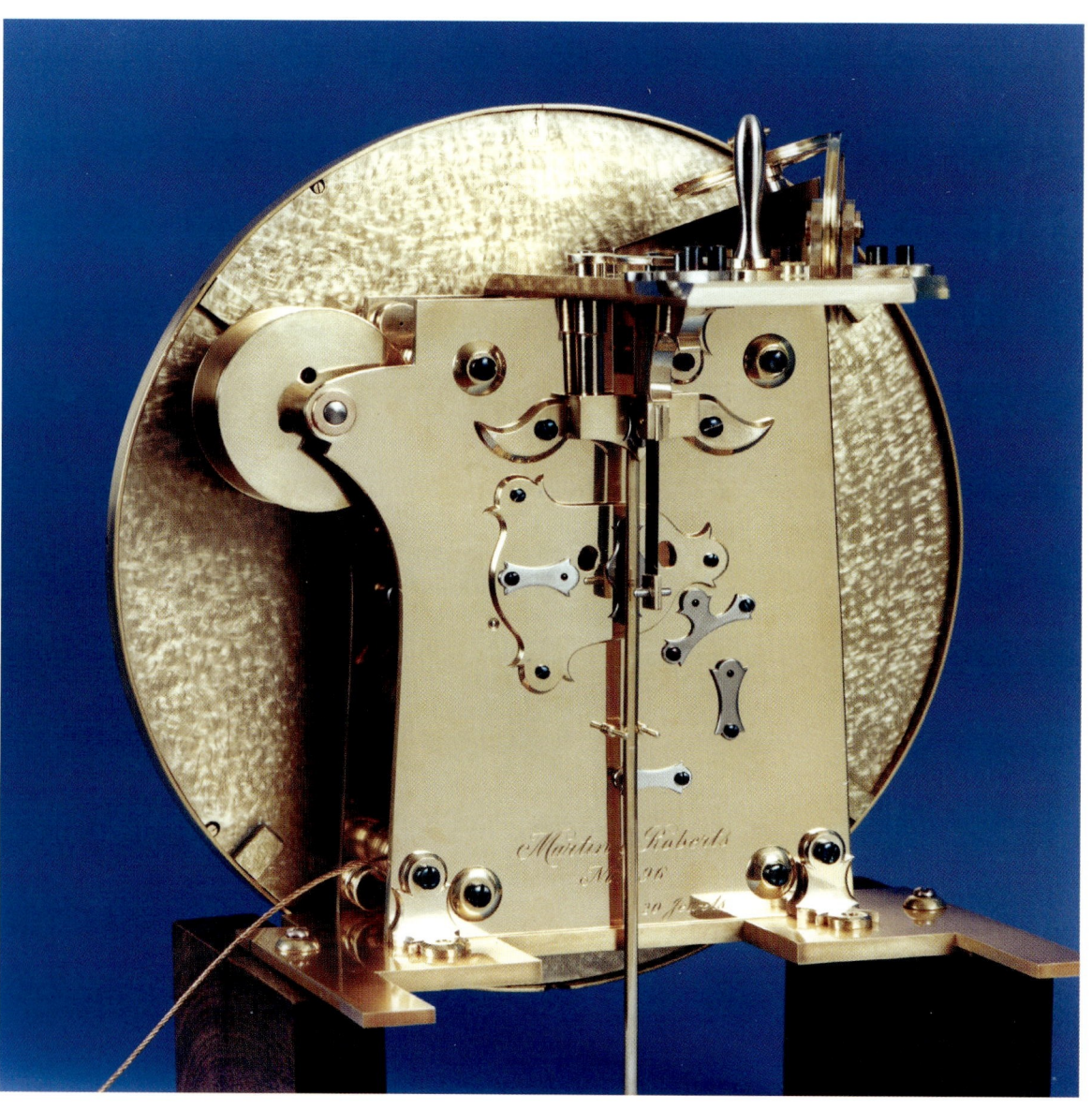

Figure 12b. **The fully jewelled movement.** The pulley system at the top was devised to ensure that the weight drops exactly vertically with its felt covered back just touching the backboard.

Technical Description of the Martin & Roberts Regulators

Eight Day & Month Clocks

The basic design of all these Martin & Roberts regulators is essentially the same. They are all wall clocks with a seconds pendulum suspended from a bracket on the backboard. All but the prototype, No 461, have 'ears' built onto this bracket in order to prevent the pendulum from falling in the event of a suspension failure. The pendulums all have mercurial compensation with the glass jar fitted into an adjustable stirrup to allow for coarse regulation. Fine adjustment in the later clocks is through the use of small weights on a tray above the stirrup, although some early clocks had a little tee-bar mounted across the mid-point of the pendulum rod, which in turn , carried weights. This however was found to be too coarse a method of adjustment.

The mercury flasks are all held in place by their own weight and fit into a brass cover plate. The early ones were all open at the top in line with much of 19th century practice, but the later ones were closed with a stainless steel bush and screwed plug which, in turn, locates into a hole in the centre of the brass top cover.

Eight day clocks are provided with a five-pound weight, whereas a seven pound weight is used for those of month duration. The pendulum, weight, pulley & winding key are all engraved M&R & numbered.

Unlike English regulator practice all the clocks produced by the partnership have centre sweep seconds, minute & hour hands. The round dial clocks have their dials silvered and are provided with a silvered cast bezel. The multi-dial clocks all have the main raised chapter ring in the arch with, below it and to either side, subsidiary dials for the month & the days of the month. Above six o'clock in the main chapter ring is a lunar calendar, seen through a cut-out in the matted brass dial centre and below the main ring is a rotating dial depicting the days of the week and their ruling dieties, seen through a seven spoke spider. In each bottom corner of the dial plate is an oval cut-out in which engraved cyphers can be displayed. On all the calendar clocks the dial plates are decoratively engraved, as are the components of the pendulum, the weight and the pulley.

All the eight day movements have 5" square plates with four screwed pillars, whereas the month clocks have 6" high plates with the sides shaped to embrace the extra wheel-work and employ six pillars. All the clocks employ a Graham deadbeat escapement and the wheel-work has six crossings. The train count is as follows:

Great wheel	120	10
1st wheel	80	10
2nd wheel	75	10
Escape wheel	30	

To provide for month duration a further wheel of 80 is interposed after the great wheel, the latter meshing with a pinion of 16 and the second pinion being changed from 10 to 12. In addition the escape wheel and pallets are scaled down to three-quarters size.

The pivot holes of the movement are jewelled with rubies and provided with end-stones, held captive under steel plates and the pallets are jewelled with agate.

The later clocks have double click-work and all are provided with Harrison's maintaining power and beat adjustment.

The escape wheel arbor is led through the front plate to carry the centre sweep seconds hand and passes through a pipe, flanged to screw to the front-plate, and having a jewel hole fitted to its outer end.

The drive to the motion work is taken through the front plate by an extended arbor from the first wheel (second in the case of a month clock). This carries, friction-tight, a wheel of 45 which drives through a similar idle wheel to a cannon pinion, also of 45, which runs on the pipe carrying the second arbor.

The idle wheel is supported in a cock and the hour wheel runs on a conventional bridge astride the cannon pinion.

The earlier clocks met with some criticism due to the inevitable backlash which was present through the train of wheels driving the minute hand. To overcome this two idle wheels were employed with the teeth of each lightly spring-loaded against the other, thus taking up most of the slack at the mesh points.

All the multi-dial calendar clocks are of month duration and, when first designed, the operating mechanism was of the simple kind, i.e. it assumed that each month had 31 days. Clocks numbered 475, 476 & 490 were built in this way; however before long 475 was altered to have a perpetual calendar. The first production clock made to this design was No 491 but unfortunately this had shortcomings in the four year mechanism governing the leap years. Thus this was re-designed and the modifications incorporated in No 475 for testing purposes and proved in practice. Following this Nos. 476 & 491 were up-dated and all subsequent clocks of this type fitted with this mechanism. This thus left No 490 as the only clock with simple calendar-work.

The Year Clock No. 496

Totally different to all the others, this clock has a wood rod pendulum with a large fully engraved and gilded brass bob which is suspended from a bridge which spans the top of the plates and rests on a bracket fixed to the backboard. This bridge also carries a system of pulleys over which the line runs so that the 24 lb weight, which is also engraved and gilded, can be wound up fully behind the movement to give the maximum possible fall of 48".

The movement incorporates Harrison's maintaining power, double click-work and is fully jewelled, together with jewelled pallets.

Year duration movements require great care in assembly as the plates are large and heavy and there are lots of arbors with delicate pivots, which particularly applies to the escape wheel arbor. In order to simplify this problem the escape arbor and that of the fifth wheel have their rear pivots running in a sub-plate through a cut-out in the backplate. With this removed these arbors can be installed and withdrawn without disturbing the rest of the train. For fine adjustment of the pallet depths the front jewel for the pallet arbor pivot is mounted in a slide which is provided with vertical screw adjustment, after which it can be locked into place.

The 10" diameter hard enamelled dial is set with half opals and gold paillons. The centre seconds and year calendar hands are of blued steel and the minute and hour hands made of pierced and gilded brass. The dial is set into an ornamental gilded cast brass bezel.

Performance

When the partners first set about designing these clocks the object was not to produce a regulator of great accuracy. The possibility to do that was immediately sacrificed by reducing the mass of all the components and thereby losing a lot of the rigidity inherent in the true English regulator. The principal object was to produce a hybrid, a clock of beauty which would grace any home, even a small apartment, but combine in it all the best practice to be found in 19th century English regulator design.

Having said that, over the years reports filtered back to the partners of accuracy as high as plus or minus one second in three months. Certainly a second over three weeks is obtainable and plus or minus one second a week would be normal.

Perhaps surprisingly there would appear to be no significant difference in performance between the simple eight day clock and those of month duration and with full perpetual calendar, despite the variable loads with which the movement of the latter would have to cope.

Martin and Roberts regulators were all commissioned and built in an era when the mechanical pendulum clock had ceased to be used for accurate timekeeping, but it is hoped that they will continue to give pleasure, even if, day-to-day, our lives are not regulated by them.

BASIC SPECIFICATION (opposite page):
1) **Numbering System.** This was started with the first two numbers, 46, which was the age of the partners when Martin & Roberts was formed. To this was added: 1 for the first clock ie. 461. Thereafter all the clocks with their pendulums, weights and pulleys were numbered sequentially, 462, 463, etc.
2) **Pendulums.** All were mercury compensated, the first few having open, and the remainder sealed glass jars.
3) **Escapements.** A dead beat escapement with jewelled pallets was used on all clocks.
4) **Jewelling.** This was employed for the escape wheel and pallet arbors and also to provide end stones. In all, 15 were used in each clock.
5) **Maintaining power.** Harrisons' design, together with beat regulation, was employed throughout the production run.

CLOCK No.	PURCHASER	ORDER DATE	SPECIFICATION	CABINET MAKER	SALE PRICE
461	Mrs. A.H. Martin, Sevenoaks, Kent	May 1978	Prototype. Walnut case. Ref "Clock of the month" Clocks magazine Sept 1978.	E.R.Truphet, Borough Green	£1,500
462	Columbia Clock Co., Michigan U.S.A	March 1979	Month clock, round dial, Rosewood case	E,R.Truphet.	£2,030
463	Lister Marketing, Sevenoaks, Kent	April 1978	8 day clock, round dial, Mahogany case	E.R.Truphet.	£1,728
464	Lister Marketing, Sevenoaks, Kent	July 1978	8 day clock, round dial, Mahogany case	E.R.Truphet.	£1,975
465	Mr. B.C Gothard, Pembury, Kent	May 1978	8 day clock, round dial, Mahogany case	E.R.Truphet.	£1,736
466	Professor E.E.J. Kirk, Dunedin, N.Z.	April 1978	8 day clock, round dial, Mahogany case	E.R.Truphet.	£1,600
467	Herr Jedermann, Germany	March 1979	8 day clock, round dial, Mahogany case	E.R.Truphet.	£2,050
468	Lister Marketing, Sevenoaks, for Wempe, Germany.	June 1978	8 day clock, round dial, Mahogany case	E.R.Truphet.	£2,050
469	Mr. A. Wilson, Aylesbury, Bucks	June 1978	8 day clock, round dial, Rosewood case	E.R.Truphet.	£2,450
470	Mr. J.D.K. Watson, Buckinghamshire	June 1978	8 day clock, round dial, Walnut case	E.R.Truphet.	£2,450
471	Mr. H. Vogel, Dusseldorf, Germany	June 1978	8 day clock, round dial, Rosewood case	E.R.Truphet.	£2,050
472	Lister Marketing, Sevenoaks, Kent for Wempe, Germany	August 1978	8 day clock, round dial, Mahogany case	E.R.Truphet.	£2,050
473	Mr W.Mitchell, Sutton Coldfield, through Michael Cox	August 1978	8 day clock, round dial, Rosewood case	E.R.Truphet.	£2,050
474	Mr. A.C.S. Medlock, Scotland	Sept 1978	8 day clock, round dial, Rosewood case	E.R.Truphet.	£2,450
475	J.S. Martin		Month, multi-dial, Walnut case, Prototype	E.R.Truphet.	
476	D.H. Roberts		Month, multi-dial, Satinwood, Prototype	E.R.Truphet.	
477	Mr. E.W. Kelsey, Essex	August 1978	8 day clock, round dial, Mahogany case, later converted to month duration	E.R.Truphet.	£2,450
478	Lister Marketing, Sevenoaks, Kent	June 1978	8 day clock, round dial, Mahogany case	E.R.Truphet.	£2,042
479	Col. Claridge, E. Grinstead	Nov 1978	8 day clock, round dial, Rosewood case	E.R.Truphet.	£2,700
480	Herr. Huber, Germany	Nov 1978	8 day clock, round dial, Mahogany case	E.R.Truphet.	£2,500
481	Mr. R. Kahrmann, London for Niederost, Switzerland	Nov 1978	8 day clock, round dial, Rosewood case	E.R.Truphet.	£2,750
482	Made for stock, sold to Mr Odell, Croydon. Exhibited Basle Fair.	May 1985	8 day clock, round dial, Walnut case	Wilkinson.	£2,750
483	Mr.H.C. Gibson, Florida, U.S.A	May 1980	8 day clock, round dial, Rosewood case	Wilkinson.	£2,750
484	Lister Marketing, Sevenoaks.	Nov 1978	8 day clock, round dial, Mahogany case	E.R.Truphet.	£2,750
485	Mr. Buttifant, Sutton Valence, Kent	Nov 1978	8 day clock, round dial, Mahogany case	E.R.Truphet.	£2,750
486	Mr. W.D. Carruthers, Germany	Nov 1978	8 day clock, round dial, Mahogany case	E.R.Truphet.	£2,750
487	Lister Marketing, Sevenoaks, Kent	November 1978	8 day clock, round dial, Mahogany case	E.R.Truphet.	£2,500
488	Mr. D.B. Palmer, Hawkhurst, Kent	June 1979	8 day clock, round dial, Walnut case	E.R.Truphet.	£2,700
489	Made for stock. Sold J.Martin, partner at close of business	1981	8 day clock, round dial, Rosewood case	Wilkinson.	
490	Asprey & Co., London	January 1982	Month, multi-dial clock, Walnut case, Simple calendar-work.	E.R.Truphet.	£6,375
491	Mr. H. Gold, Los Angeles, U.S.A. Subsequently acquired Bill Taylor.	August 1983	Month, multi-dial clock, mahogany case, with perpetual calendar-work.	E.R.Truphet.	£11,500
492	Mr. F. De Ramer, New Hampshire, U.S.A. Via Ray Bates.	September 1987	Month, multi-dial clock, perpetual calendar, and Satinwood case	E.R.Truphet.	$25,000
493	Mr. A. McDowall, Kent	January 1991	Month, multi-dial, perpetual calendar and Satinwood case with inlaid backboard	Nick Martin Lincolnshire.	£16,400
494	Mr. J. Henley, Kent. Ordered By Wyatt, Bough Beech, who defaulted.	January 1991	Month, multi-dial, perpetual calendar and Mahogany case	Nick Martin Lincolnshire.	£16,400
495	D.H. Roberts		Prototype year duration clock in rose-wood case.	E.R.Truphet.	
496	Mr. J. Maynard	Jan 1995	Only production year duration clock with rosewood case.	C.Buckwell. Derek Roberts Antiques.	£45,000
497	Mr. P. Fowler, London	July 1992	Month duration round dial mahogany case & engraved pendulum. (Now in New Zealand)	C.Buckwell. Derek Roberts Antiques.	£15,000
498	Mr. P.H. Martin, Sussex	January 1997	Month duration clock, round dial, Rosewood case. (This clock is now in Australia)	Nick Martin Lincolnshire.	£14,500

Chapter 5

Finance and Property

In our early days as and when the neighbouring properties to us became available around 30 years ago, we bought them at very modest prices, and they proved, in every sense, to be a good investment. They were also good collateral if we wanted to borrow money but did not want to compromise in any way the security of our business or home. When times are difficult, the advantages of having a business in the country in premises you own and where expenses are relatively low has much to recommend it.

Figure 13. **E M Mallinson's painting** of 22-30 Shipbourne Road, circa 1950. The properties are, from right to left: 22, 23 which were fully restored and became an antiques centre; 24 which was our first showroom and home; 25 our final showroom; 26 a shop, and 27, which was run as an antiques centre and finally became our son's business premises.

Figure 14. **Nos 22-23 Shipbourne Road**, which became Tudor Cottage Antiques.

Fairly soon after we started up, we had the chance to buy no. 22 Shipbourne Road (figure 13), a semi-detached 15th century cottage next door but one to us and the price agreed was £1,750; however, the deal nearly fell through at the last minute when the vendor realised that he would have to pay £75 tax. I offered to pay this for him and all was well. A few years later no. 23, which was attached to no. 22, also came onto the market, but by then the price had risen somewhat and we had to pay £2,650. This gave us the chance to totally restore the two buildings for which, some years later, we were given a civic society award (figure 14).

There were three further properties we were to become involved in; no. 27 Shipbourne Road, which initially could only be leased. It was run as an antiques centre to try and increase the interest in antiques in this area and was later transferred to our son, Stuart, who finally purchased it and ran his security business from there.

Our last but one purchase of local premises was a spacious flat immediately above our premises. I used it as an office and for storing some of the clocks awaiting restoration or the overflow from the showroom; however, I found that the separation of my office from the main showroom, etc downstairs was a mistake. We thus obtained planning permission to join the two together and put an extension on one side; however, this

was never to happen. By that time we had bought another house to live in and ended up selling it.

Once the business could be seen to be doing well we had several offers of money to put into it. This, in many ways, appeared to be attractive as the more money and thus stock you have, the greater the turnover that can be achieved and there is no particular reason why it should increase the expenses too much. I had seen this approach adopted by several dealers and with one notable example I can call to mind, it proved very successful; however, we had come into the world of antiques because we enjoyed the way of life and did not want to put any undue pressure on ourselves. If I made a mistake when I bought something, then I would accept the loss and there was an end to it, but if I had bought it on behalf of someone else it would have been a different matter. Nobody likes losing money.

In the world of art and antiques, it doesn't matter at what level you deal, you can still run out of money. Many years ago a friend of mine in the art world had authority to write out a cheque for up to four million pounds with a total budget of seventeen and occasionally he still had to ask for more money. The big advantage of having limited resources is that you buy very carefully, whereas if you have no such restrictions, you may, for instance, buy a fine piece because you like it, but at a price too high to be able to sell it at a profit.

As mentioned earlier, the business started with a capital, excluding the premises, of £5,000 and this was regularly raised by ploughing back much of the profits. We could afford to do this because I did, at that time, have another source of income and our standard of living, by choice, was relatively modest.

We did also use bank money when we felt it was justified and it never, in any way, put the business at risk. We found that we could achieve a return on the value of the stock of around 35% gross per annum and thus if we borrowed money at, say 6-7% to increase the value of the stock and thus the turnover, the risk was very small and the benefits substantial; however, another lesson learnt was that the more stock you carry the slower its turnover.

The classic (and extreme) example of this is the runner who just sells to the trade and tries to turn over his stock as soon as he has acquired it and never gets involved in any restoration. He may not turn it over weekly, but some of them probably averaged a turnover time of two weeks, ie 25 times per year. The only slight problem the runner will face is that if he, for instance, buys ten items a week and sells nine, then gradually the number 10s will accumulate and in the end he will be forced to try and dispose of them, either at cost or a small loss, or in part exchange deals, otherwise he will end up with all his capital tied up in no. 10s.

The contrast to this is the successful West End dealer who may, because he has to have a range of the finest pieces to tempt his wealthy clients, have many millions of pounds tied up in stock. All will have been carefully selected, researched and restored, and this can easily run into a year or two. He then has to wait until a suitable client comes in who will pay him the price he now needs to cover the time involved and the very high expense of running the business. It may thus be that it is two to three years before he has finally recouped his original investment. This may be a reasonable proposition in good times, with rising prices and indeed substantial profits made in the past, but recently the situation has become untenable for some prestigious businesses such as Aspreys, Garrard and Partridges, to name but three.

Although no business is ever completely free of risk, we found that once the turnover got into seven figures and we were making reasonable profit margins we had no problems, that is until the last recession, roughly from 1989-92, when property prices crashed, maybe 40%, and interest rates went up to 16-17%.

We had been looking for a property for a couple of years as we felt we would, after over 20 years, like to live away from the business; however, we had seen nothing which enticed us and now, as there were clear signs of a recession on the horizon, we had decided to pull out of the market.

It was at this stage that an agent phoned and said that the sale of a house which she thought was ideal for us had just fallen through and she strongly advised us to go and see it, and this we agreed to do, despite our earlier decision. An appointment was arranged and phoned through to us, but, unfortunately, we never received the message. The agent thus contacted us the next day to query why we hadn't gone to see the house and we explained that we knew nothing about it. Another time was agreed and we duly went to see it.

Unfortunately or fortunately, depending on ones point of view, it proved to be exactly what we were looking for. It was a perfect early autumn evening and the sun was beginning to go down on what must be one of the best outlooks in Kent. I had been walking the hills in which the house was set for many years, at least in part because of the excellent views, but had never thought I would be able to buy a house looking out onto them.

We discussed the price, which seemed quite modest, relative to the property and garden, but were still nervous of the oncoming recession, particularly as I would have to sell three of my properties in Tonbridge to cover it. I said that we were seriously interested but would have to discuss it with our estate agent and the bank. I approached the estate agent first who said that he thought there would be little difficulty in selling the three properties in Tonbridge which were not required for the business and that they should fetch considerably more than the amount we had to raise.

My next port of call was the bank manager and here I will divert a little. I had had an account with Lloyds for maybe 25 years and during that time no problem had ever arisen; however, recently the manager had changed and the new one asked me in to see him. He was by no means suitable for the job and asked me, with little ado, to see my previous accounts which I had actually already submitted to the bank, as was my habit, at the end of each financial year.

He then asked for weekly sales and other figures. I explained that these would be of little value as our business was such that I could take as much money in a day as I had in the previous month; however, he was not to be placated and said that he would withdraw the bank's facilities unless the figures were provided. I did not argue with him further, but walked across the road to the National Westminster and saw the manager there, explained what properties I owned and discussed the business. I then asked him if he would like to take over the accounts. The business was highly regarded in Tonbridge and he didn't hesitate. All I specified was that I didn't want it to incur me in any expense and that the charges were at least as low as Lloyds and, in fact, they turned out to be somewhat less. I signed the release papers and all proceeded smoothly. I learnt afterwards the Lloyds manager lost the bank several important customers in Tonbridge.

A surprising incident, shortly before I left Lloyds, was that the bank mistakenly posted me confidential reports on some six local businesses, some of them quite scathing. When I asked the manager if he had lost any such papers, he strongly denied it. I then gave them back to him, for which I received no thanks.

It was subsequently suggested by the National Westminster that the management of the account be transferred to their business centre with whom I built up an excellent relationship and it was to them that I turned to seek advice on the house. The manager came over to view it with me and was strongly of the opinion that I should buy it. I asked the obvious question as to what would happen if I had not sold my other properties when I was due to complete and he assured me that that would not be a problem.

Unfortunately, Valerie and I had virtually a love affair with the house which had everything we wanted and thus had decided to buy it, so went back to the owner to discuss the matter further. It turned out that he did not really want or even need to move for about a year as he had bought some land in Cyprus and was building a house there; however, he needed some money to put towards the building costs. It was thus agreed that I would pay him a £100,000 on exchange of contracts and complete one year later.

The £100,000 was duly paid and our properties put in the hands of the agents, but despite much interest and a gradual reduction of the prices, no firm sales were forthcoming. One friend said that he would buy the main property at the end of the year and that the money was in the bank but, unfortunately, the bank didn't agree with him.

The completion day came and as I was a sole trader I took some of the money back from the business which I had invested in it, with the agreement of the bank, and let the overdraft soar; not a particularly comfortable situation. It was at this stage that I discussed the matter with a customer and friend who was a very shrewd businessman. His immediate advice was to reduce the price of the properties by 20%, when they were bound to sell. I would then be in a position to concentrate on the business and enjoy my home.

It was very good advice, which, after discussing the matter with the estate agents, sadly I did not take as they felt that the market had bottomed out and they were close to finding suitable buyers. This proved to be far from the case and with interest rates still rising, I decided to reduce my overdraft by other means to ease the substantial interest the business was paying the bank.

I had, maybe 30 years before, built up a small portfolio of shares worth around £3,000. In this I was possibly trying to follow in my father's footsteps who had made substantial sums of money on the stock exchange, but only by studying and following certain areas very carefully. This I had not done and had achieved little more than, overall, maintain the value of the shares.

As I had no interest in stocks and shares, I sold them and put the money into clocks and I now sold half of these and they realised around £150,000; my first steps in the reduction of the overdraft. I also disposed of some other antiques.

It is at this stage that another unfortunate, or perhaps I should say untimely, event occurred. About ten years earlier I had obtained the occupation of very good workshop premises only 100 yards from the shop by purchasing the bankrupt business of Crutch brothers. I hate leasing premises and had, on several occasions, tried to buy it from the Trust who owned it but for a variety of reasons failed to do so. For instance in one case a member of the Trust who was keen to sell died and the sale fell through. On the last occasion, some two years earlier, I had made a substantial offer for the entire site, as they refused to sell just the barn I was interested in. This comprised two detached 16th century cottages in much need of attention, a barn, a milking parlour, another outbuilding, several garages,

a garden and a potential building plot; however, they refused my offer. Now, out of the blue, they said they would accept it. I pointed out that this was 2 years ago and before the recession had started and that prices had fallen by up to 40% since then. In view of this I could now only offer 40% less than on the last occasion. They would not quite accept this offer, maybe on principle, but settled for an extra £5,000. I did have the advantage of being a sitting tenant with the bulk of the lease still to run, which meant that it would have been quite difficult to sell the property to someone else.

There was no problem as far as the bank was concerned, indeed they were quite enthusiastic, and the architect thought that the planning application for a substantial house on the plot should present no problem, and so we went ahead.

In this instance the old saying that if you have a problem then sometimes it is better to add another one to it proved to be correct.

The purchase of the land gave rear access and parking spaces for the three properties we were trying to sell and made it much easier to dispose of them. Once rear access to our property was created, the neighbours quickly approached us and bought rights of way from us, and the garages which were surplus to requirements were disposed of. Building plots always seem to be much in demand and once planning was approved this sold easily, and the cottage which needed most attention went to a builder, who renovated it for his daughter.

By now we had recouped most of our initial outlay and we still had the stable block with the building behind it, which gave us all the space we needed. We also had the milking parlour, a most attractive old building, which proved to be perfect for me as a photographic studio, and one old cottage which we reserved for my son and his future wife. The entire saga had taken some 4-5 years, but at the end of it all the business was in a stronger position and we had the house of our own dreams. Thereafter the business continued to do well.

Chapter 6
Robberies, Thefts & Stolen Clocks

In the early days, security was, in hindsight, amazingly lax. We just had a bell fixed to the front door which sounded, quite loudly, when anyone came in. This might be when either Greig Dallimore or one of us was in the shop, but could equally well be when we were upstairs and had to hurry down.

We went on in this way for several years until the first of our thefts occurred. A couple came into the showroom, looked around, asked a few questions and then left. My wife went upstairs and when the bell went again a few minutes later hurried down again, only to see the girl who had been in the shop a little earlier, making towards the door with a carriage clock and a chronometer. Valerie gave chase but the girl leapt into the car which was outside with its engine running and it drove off; however, we did record the number.

We phoned the police, and gave them details of the car and the direction it was heading in the hope that they might be able to intercept it, but this was a forlorn hope. About 40 minutes later a constable appeared and produced the forms which had to be filled in. These seemed to require as much detail of Valerie and me as they did of the criminals.

About a week later, we received a phone call from the police saying that they thought they knew the man involved, but needed Valerie's help and would she kindly assist with an identikit. When Valerie got to the police station she explained that it was the girl whom she had seen most of and could identify best; however, this was of little assistance as they only had an identikit for men at that time and one for women was a long way off; before that they had to produce them for men of Indian or Afro-Caribbean origin.

Valerie managed to achieve a reasonably good likeness and a few days later they asked if she would come with them to identify the man, who lived in Greenwich. She asked what would happen if she did decide it was the person involved in the robbery. She was told he would be arrested and brought back to Tonbridge with them and that she would have to sit in the back seat with him, which was something she did not relish and so decided to go up in the Morris Minor on her own and then transfer to the police car. The idea was to wait until he came out of the house, when Valerie could identify him or not as the case might be.

Several hours passed with Valerie sitting alongside a large policeman in the front seat who was unfortunately becoming increasingly amorous and had to be discouraged. With no one

leaving the house, the police decided to knock on the door and when he emerged Valerie positively identified him. The police arrested him and drove off and Valerie was left to find her own way back to Tonbridge.

I arrived home around 7 o'clock, but no Valerie and by 9 o'clock I was getting increasingly worried so phoned the police who, unfortunately, could give me no information at all. Around 10.30 that night Valerie finally turned up to regale me with her experiences of the day.

The case duly came to court and he pleaded guilty, which saved Valerie having to attend. Before sentencing he pleaded that it would result in great hardship if he was sent to prison as not only had he a wife with three children to support but a girlfriend who was eight months pregnant as well.

He was given a 6 months suspended sentence. The chronometer was spotted in a street market and recovered, but we never saw the carriage clock again.

The Baby in the Carry Cot

A young couple came in one day with a well wrapped-up baby just a few months old. They spent some time looking at the Tunbridge-Ware and left after maybe half an hour. It was unfortunately a little while before we realised that a carriage clock and another small clock had disappeared beneath the baby.

The Man with the Pipe

The next three incidents which occurred were not of any great consequence, but quite upsetting. The first of these was a man who spent quite a long time looking at all the clocks in detail, whilst smoking a pipe which he was frequently poking with a gadget similar to a penknife. During the time he was in the shop a couple of other customers came in whom we talked to and after maybe an hour he left.

Some time later, I noticed that the key was missing from the back of a 17th century bracket clock. I asked Valerie if she knew where it was, but she could not help and on opening the door, I realised that the lock was missing also. We then checked the other bracket clocks and found that he had stolen the locks out of three of these as well.

The disappointment was not so much the theft as such, but that the originality of four fine early clocks could be harmed for so little gain.

The Tunbridge-Ware Samples

At the time in question, we were carrying an extensive stock of Tunbridge-Ware and had been fortunate enough to acquire a set of veneers, sample blocks, slices, etc, which showed exactly how it was made. These were kept on a couple of shelves with some notes for everyone's benefit so that they could understand the method of construction.

A Tunbridge-Ware collector came in, looked at the various pieces we had for sale and then asked how much the sample pieces were. I explained that they were not for sale, and indeed they were clearly marked as such, but for everyone's benefit. He would not accept this and said they must have a price, but I explained again that it was not a matter of money but of interest.

Shortly after this I became involved with a party of overseas visitors and during this time he left and with him went the Tunbridge-Ware samples, although I didn't realise it at the time. The disappointment, apart from the fact that anyone should do such a thing, was that, although their monetary value was not high, they were virtually irreplaceable.

The crimes committed so far were not of a violent nature, and had not been of any great consequence, and we had taken some measures, such as a panic alarm system and remote door opening, to try and make the premises more secure and had fitted ornamental, but strong, grilles to the side windows.

We had transferred the business to no. 25 and were living at no. 24 Shipbourne Road when the next incident occurred. There was a loud noise of smashing glass from the showroom. I grabbed a dressing gown, rushed down and entered the back of no. 25, only to see the robber going out through the broken glass of the front door. By the time I got out of the shop he had disappeared down a lane some yards away; however, he dropped a cosh, which was a short iron bar with a ball of lead on it, so it was probably just as well that I didn't catch up with him.

Carriage Clocks & Switzerland

At the time this incident occurred we were selling quite a lot of carriage clocks to Switzerland, particularly the finer and rarer pieces and had sold nine such clocks to a collector, mostly quite recognisable ones.

We arranged for one of the major shippers, who did runs to Switzerland every week, to take them out for us and usually they were there within a matter of days, but in this instance they did not arrive. The shippers were informed and all the documentation checked. They had left London on time, were cleared as the van went into Holland and cleared again when they entered Germany, but there was no trace of them passing into Switzerland. It was at that stage, with enquiries continuing, that we received a phone call from a local clockmaker to let us know that a batch of rare carriage clocks had appeared in a shop in Maidstone which we might be interested in. When he described them it was obvious that they were the clocks

we had had stolen, but how they ended up there we could not imagine.

We informed the police and arranged for Roger Lister, who worked for us at the time, to go over and see the clocks, and once he had positively identified them, to let them know. They would be waiting outside in plain clothes and would then come in and take over. Things did not quite go according to plan. Roger arrived at the shop around 3.30pm and asked to see the clocks which a friend had seen there. They said that they knew nothing about them and he would have to wait until the owner returned. Some time later they started to pull down the shutters and lock the front door, which, with Roger inside, worried the police and they forced an entry.

At this stage the carriage clocks were forthcoming and they explained they had bought them, at what seemed an extremely modest price, from a lady who lived in Folkestone whose name and address they supplied. The police took the carriage clocks away, which we had already shown them photos of and went to visit the lady.

It emerged that her husband was a lorry driver and that he had bought them from another English lorry driver he knew when they met up at a transport café near Switzerland. That lorry driver was due back in Dover on the following Monday and the police were waiting for him, but he never arrived and indeed apparently never returned to this country.

The carriage clocks were returned to us, completely undamaged and a week later had started on their journey to Switzerland again. Nobody was ever prosecuted.

A couple of years later another batch of carriage clocks on their way to Switzerland, but this time by air, also went missing. They were eventually found in Sri Lanka; someone had forgotten to take them off the plane when it landed in Zurich on its way there. Two days later they reached the client.

The Motorbike Incident

We were discussing an early bracket clock with a couple one afternoon when a motorbike drove up onto the pavement; the pillion rider leapt off the back, sledgehammer in hand, smashed the window, grabbed the clock on display, and roared off before I could reach them. They had obviously done their homework well as they immediately turned right and went down a pathway which led through to the main road below. The mess was cleared up and all the glass changed to armoured which, I was assured, would withstand such an attack.

A similar incident occurred in Bond Street shortly afterwards. A motorbike came to an abrupt stop outside one of the leading jewellers; the pillion rider immediately leapt off and started attacking the window with his sledgehammer. Unfortunately for him, the harder he hit the window the faster the sledgehammer bounced back, infuriating him and making the attack even more frenzied. As this went on a crowd gathered round to watch and found it most amusing. In the end he gave up in disgust, threw down the sledgehammer, leapt on the back of the bike and roared off. Nobody made any attempt to detain him.

It was in the late 80s to early 90s that ram-raids came onto the scene. The main targets seeming to be jewellers and antique dealers with all the raids probably being organised by one gang at any one time. A friend of mine in Westerham had three ram-raids in 18 months, a particularly frightening experience if you are living over or behind the shop. After the third incident he gave up and moved to Spain. He was probably unlucky in that he was in an ideal site so far as they were concerned, being close to the motorway and with five different roads leading out of the town.

Another friend had an attempted ram-raid when the thieves used a railway sleeper fixed inside the boot of a car. This failed but they were back some months later and this time used a lorry to devastating effect. They even removed a heavy safe unopened which was found with the door open in a field some miles away a few days later.

We had thought that we might escape as the Shipbourne Road is quite narrow and it would be fairly easy for the police to block either end; however, there were no police stationed near us and the robbers probably knew they had plenty of time to play with.

All the bracket and carriage clocks were locked in a large safe at the back of the premises so the value of the individual items available to them was not particularly high. They stole all our barometers, some wall clocks, bracket clocks of lesser value and all the Tunbridge-Ware, adding up in total to around £45,000; however, they did leave several smashed clocks on the floor which was a sad sight to see and broken glass everywhere.

Once again we had to review security. Already we had built a large brick flowerbed about 3 feet high in front of the window so that they could not ram-raid there and we also had grilles in front of the windows. Now we had to install heavy steel bars which were bolted across the door every night and also put in 24-hour security cameras.

This series of ram-raids, almost certainly done by the same gang, died down, presumably because they finally fell foul of the law, but started again, even more violently, maybe five years later and this time even included an attack on a museum. In this instance, it is thought they were commissioned, for a set fee, to steal a specific clock, but unfortunately miscalculated and broke into the wrong part of the building and had to content themselves with some lesser pieces.

This gang was eventually, after many incidents, spotted leaving a town near Chippenham after a raid. They were followed by police who managed to get vehicles in front of and behind them as they approached the Hammersmith flyover. On the flyover the car in front jammed on its brakes and the one behind stopped hard behind. A fight ensued, after which I believe two policemen had to go to hospital, and one of the crooks then amazingly jumped over the edge of the parapet and was seen crawling away below.

At the committal proceedings they were given bail and disappeared. One was subsequently rearrested when he was involved in an armed Post Office raid in which someone was shot. The police received a phone call from the Spanish authorities regarding one of the others. Evidently he had been caught smuggling drugs into Spain from North Africa. They were asked if they wanted to institute extradition proceedings at this stage, but they declined saying that they would rather wait until he had served his sentence in Spain.

The last unfortunate incident we were involved in was on a Saturday morning. We made the mistake of letting someone in, in a hooded duffle coat which concealed much of his face. All we could do at that stage was watch him closely. When he asked to leave we breathed a sigh of relief and pressed the button, releasing the door for him to go out. He opened the door, walked halfway through and then, with one foot holding the door, wheeled round and grabbed the nearest clock before dashing out. I rushed after him, a little behind as I had to open the door again and raced up the road as he ran to his car. The street was busy and I called out for people to apprehend him, including two burly 6th form boys, but nobody moved. I grabbed him as he got into the car, but was unable to stop him as he drove off, with me half in and half out of the car. With traffic approaching from the other direction I was likely to become the meat in the sandwich and so let go and dropped into the road. Very bravely a youngster jumped onto the back of the escaping car, but was thrown off at the next roundabout, which the thief negotiated at high speed, knocking two other cars out of the way in the process.

I arrived back at the shop looking more than a little disreputable, my fall onto the road doing my clothes (and me)! no good at all, with large tears and holes in my trousers and thick sports coat, which luckily I was wearing. It was at that moment that two immaculately dressed Americans came into the shop by appointment to see me. They concealed their surprise at my appearance remarkably well and it was at that stage that Valerie thought she should offer some explanation!

The police arrived shortly afterwards. We gave details of the car and as the thief made the mistake of looking straight at the video camera we had some good shots of him. The police seemed to know something of him and thought that he came from Brighton, but despite this, nothing further was heard.

As on all previous occasions, the loss adjuster appeared on the scene the next day and within a short time the claim had been settled.

Stolen Goods

There are two things that concern a dealer above almost anything; the first is buying something which is stolen and, even worse, selling it.

We were fortunate in that over the 37 years of trading we can only recall buying three stolen items. Probably the best way of guarding against this is to only buy from the vendor's home, unless you know them well and to always pay by cheque so that, if necessary, the person who sold the item to you can be traced.

In the first instance, the customer had been referred to us from a reputable dealer whom we had known for several years, but did not deal in carriage clocks, and for that reason we were happy to buy a carriage clock off him; however, it did turn out that he had only met the dealer once. It was another dealer who realised that it was a clock which one of his customers had lost and we thus returned the carriage clock to him. All attempts to trace the person who sold us the clock failed.

On the second occasion, I asked another dealer to represent us at the auction of a year duration wall regulator by Dent which was coming up for sale in the Midlands, minus its pendulum. This was a complex one, but fortunately we had had another such clock through our hands before and were reasonably certain that we could make an exact copy of the pendulum.

The work was completed some six months later and the clock photographed and advertised in Country Life. A lady then phoned up and said that it was her regulator which had been stolen nine months earlier. There could be no doubt on the matter as she still had the original pendulum and the clock was numbered.

She came down to see us with a police officer and it was agreed that the clock would stay with us, unsold, until matters were resolved with the auction house. They proved reluctant to accept any responsibility, initially holding the view that the matter was between us and the person who had entered the clock in the sale, and was then paid for it, but whose name and address they could not give us or the police. Their case finally collapsed, about a year later, when the owner produced a copy of a letter which she had sent to them, informing them that she had not only had the Dent stolen but also two paintings which were sold in the same sale. It was thus clear that the auctioneers had knowingly, or unwittingly, sold stolen goods and they sent me a cheque for the amount I had paid. They also had to refund on the pictures. I contacted the lady from whom the clock had been stolen and offered to check it over, deliver and set it up in her home; however, by then she was so sick of the matter that she asked me if I would buy the clock from her, so I handed over to her the sum which I received from the auction house, reunited the clock with its original pendulum and all was well.

The third occasion on which we got involved in a stolen clock was when I purchased one in Holland. I then offered the clock to a dealer in this country I knew well, only to be told that it had been stolen from a client of his some six months earlier. The clock was returned to the client, who was also known to me and in due course a refund arrived from the dealer in Holland, a little reluctantly as he felt that it should have gone back through the chain of dealers through whose hands it had passed. In this way each dealer only loses the profit he made, as opposed to the whole amount and it is just the person who bought it off the thief in the first instance who loses the whole amount, but I expect they sorted that out between them in the end.

Chapter 7

Switzerland

Until around 1980 there was a strong price differential, as far as antiques were concerned, between England and some of the European countries such as Germany where the economy was booming, Switzerland and to a somewhat lesser extent Belgium and Holland. It was thus scarcely surprising that there was a steady stream of dealers coming over from these countries.

Probably the antique dealers who benefited most were those from the home counties as the favoured port of entry was Dover. After landing there, they would usually turn left and work their way along the south coast visiting such places as Folkestone, Rye, Hastings, Bexhill and Eastbourne on the way, until they reached Brighton where at that time there was probably upwards of a hundred dealers, many carrying very extensive stocks. It was to this town that many 'runners' brought their antiques.

After this, the continental dealers would either return along the south coast, or quite often inland, maybe visiting Lewes and Tunbridge Wells and taking in various other dealers on the way. It was after this that they would sometimes call in on us at Tonbridge prior to winding their way back to Dover via the Medway Towns and Canterbury. Alternatively they might then go up to London or, if time permitted, take a tour around the West Country or go up North.

Today such tours would scarcely be practical because of the decline in country dealers, the paucity of stock and the much smaller price margins between the various countries.

We were, at this time, introduced by a West Country art dealer to a particularly interesting Englishman who had set up business in Zurich, and subsequently took up Swiss nationality. He had by no means had an easy start in life, spending his early years in a children's home.

When he was around 18, he decided to seek his fortune overseas and went to Switzerland where he found work. On his holidays back in the UK he realised that antiques were much less expensive here than in Switzerland and so took pieces back to Zurich with him to sell and before long had set himself up in business there. From then on things progressed quite rapidly. He arranged for his brother, with whom he had maintained contact, and a friend, to bring stock over from England for him. Business, because of his dedication and eagerness to learn, rapidly expanded and before too long he had moved, with a partner, into the Strehlgasse, a lovely street in the old part of Zurich.

Zurich, apart from the successful business men and bankers living there, attracts many such similar people from all over the world and thus within a relatively short time, the quantity and more particularly the quality of the antiques he was handling, rose rapidly. We continued to have a good working relationship together, although as the business expanded into other areas such as paintings, bronzes, silver and continental furniture, this gradually fell away. Now it must be the most successful business in Zurich.

An example of the international nature of the antiques world was that within a month of our selling a longcase clock to him, he had resold it, ironically, to a couple living only seven miles from us, in Sevenoaks. We even set it up for them in their home.

An even more unlikely coincidence occurred in America. When visiting New York I bought a fine clock from a couple living there and shipped it home. Within a short while after it had been checked over and the movement cleaned, we sold it to someone who lived in the same street in New York from where it came.

Times of recession could always be difficult, but such is the international nature of antiques, that there is usually one overseas market that is still buoyant. Such was the case when I was approached and asked by an agent if I could supply and deliver good quality clocks to a client of his in Switzerland. This I readily agreed to and after supplying photographs and details of various clocks, a deal was put together and I duly took the clocks out to Switzerland. Pride of place amongst these being a particularly fine English longcase regulator.

I was accompanied by John Martin, who had done many restorations for me over the years, including several of considerable complexity such as the Edward Cockey. We had also formed a partnership some years earlier to make high grade wall regulators. We decided to go down through France stopping with a friend of John's in Paris on the first night and by making an early start, reached St Louis, the French suburb of Basel, by the early afternoon.

There were three different customs entries into Switzerland through Basel at that time, all at different places and each one assigned for a different type of goods. The customs agent had advised us which entry point to go through and assured us one of his staff would be there to meet us. Unfortunately, when we arrived, no agent was there and on enquiring at the customs house, we were told that the designated customs entry for antiques had been changed two or three weeks ago. We then set off for the next customs point which sadly also turned out to be the wrong one and it was only after urgent phone calls to our agent that we finally arrived at the correct entry point, where all went well. However, by now it was getting late in the day and frantic phone calls were going too and fro between the client, his agent and our business, and we still had sixty to seventy miles to go.

Unfortunately, we arrived at his office after it had closed and as we could not contact him at his home, we went on to Arrau and spent the night there.

The next morning we met up with a rather unhappy customer, but in the end all was well and we set up the clocks, first in the offices and then in his home where we spent a very pleasant evening and departed the next morning.

Some four to five months later, the process was repeated but this time many more clocks were purchased, including one of the wall regulators which was made by the partnership of Martin & Roberts.

It was essential to use a good Swiss customs agent at that time and to get all the documentation stamped as we passed through each lot of customs on the way out. Unfortunately, our problems started with a very suspicious customs officer at Sheerness who wanted to examine every item on the documentation. We did our best to oblige him, but such was the quantity of clocks that it had been a work of art fitting them all in and thus, as far as possible, we tried to expose the items by removing blankets and packing materials. With everyone loaded on board the customs officer was still examining and searching, and it was only when the ship sounded her siren that he finally stamped the paperwork and released us. We drove rapidly to the ship, which started to raise the gangplank before we had scarcely cleared the top.

This time we used the Sheerness to Vlissingen ferry which gave a pleasant start to the journey with a magnificent spread laid up at what was called the Captains Table, a good night's sleep and an early start in the morning so that we could reach the German/Swiss border that day, and be ready to cross into Switzerland at Basel.

Thereafter all went well with our trip over to Switzerland. There was no problem at the Dutch or the German borders, and we arrived at our hotel near the Swiss border in good time for an excellent dinner with game on the menu as it was the season.

All was well the next day and we arrived in time for afternoon tea. On glancing at the regulator I had delivered six months ago, I noticed that it was accurate to the second. I asked our host how long it had taken him to bring it to such precise timekeeping, only to be told that he had not touched the clock other than to wind it since I had set it up. To dismantle a clock, transport it 400-500 miles, reassemble it and then find that it keeps virtually perfect time, must be near to a miracle which could almost certainly have influenced the

customer and helped in his decision to buy further clocks. Unfortunately, I had, to some degree, to disillusion him and explain that the other clocks we were delivering were unlikely to perform so well.

An excellent evening meal followed, accompanied by what seemed to be an endless stream of wines. Every time mine host slightly inclined his head his son disappeared and brought back from the cellar another excellent but different bottle of Swiss wine, fortunately quite light!

The next morning we went off to meet a skilled clockmaker with whom we had some contact and joined him for lunch. We explained that we had been delivering and setting up clocks and he offered to take care of them should they need any attention, but at that stage we gave him no details.

It was to be a year before we came out to Switzerland again and at this stage we had decided to exhibit at the Basel Fair, on the stand of one of the Swiss watch dealers.

One of the most impressive things was the journey to the exhibition hall. We all had to assemble around 8.00 am in groups of maybe twenty, just on the German side of the frontier and were then given a high speed non-stop police escort, right through customs and into the exhibition hall where customs clearance finally took place. It is doubtful if we ever dropped much below sixty; however, when we saw the quantity and quality of the jewellery on some of the stands, which must have been worth many millions, we understood why. The Basel Fair was a fascinating one to visit; besides all the watches, clocks and jewellery, the top floor was devoted to restaurants, each one (or more) representing a different Swiss Canton.

A particular pleasure was the presence, a little way over the border, of a fine French restaurant called Jenny's. Not only was the food excellent, but Madame knew exactly which wine, quite often a Gewürztraminer, would complement each dish. Sometimes the lot of an antique dealer is 'a hard one'!

We exhibited at Basel again the following year and at that time brought out a few more clocks for our customer; however, to improve our display and indeed to store them safely, we put these clocks on our stand at the fair. Whilst there, one of the major Swiss Museums saw a particularly fine and rare bracket clock on our stand and the next day sent their expert in to see it and then asked if they could buy it. This put us in a bit of a quandary as the clock was already sold. We tried to contact the customer, who had agreed to buy it, but had not paid us, only to find that he was away for several days, so we phoned his agent in London and explained that the Museum would give him a substantial profit on it. He immediately assured us that the customer would be delighted to take a profit on the clock and when the fair was finished, we duly delivered it to the Museum.

Unfortunately, when we visited the customer a few days after this, he had not been told by his agent that he had given instructions to sell it and was not in the least mollified by the substantial profit he had made on the deal without laying out any money.

The following year was the last time we were to do the Basel Fair. The customer had a problem with the Martin & Roberts regulator and rather than try and rectify the fault on site, we thought we would take out another identical movement and swap the two over. All our clocks were numbered and the one we took out had the next consecutive number. Unfortunately, this was to give us trouble when we left Switzerland. The meticulous Swiss had noted the number of the movement we had brought in and realised that the one we were returning with was one number different. Fortunately, in the end we managed to persuade them that all was in order.

Sadly this was not the end of our difficulties. I had taken in a part exchange deal some seventy Swiss watches, the bankrupt stock of a dealer. Evidently there were strict rules as to who was allowed to export watches from Switzerland. Lengthy debates and phone calls followed and maybe two hours later we were allowed to go on our way.

During this trip we went once more to our faithful Swiss customer and again had an excellent meal with him. This time we had a few bottles of wine and then he produced a bottle of Poire Williams, a particularly strong spirit on which he was an expert. Evidently he would get samples every year from each of the manufacturers, decide which he liked best and then order a few crates.

By about 10.30 we had finished the Poire Williams and were back on the wine again and at 12 o'clock he announced that he was going to bed as he had to leave at 6.30, as always, the next morning, to be at work by 7 o'clock; however would we please correct a fault on the French regulator on the staircase before we left. The thought of doing this filled us with horror as it would have to be done that night because the next morning we had to leave early.

The regulator in question (figure 15) was a massive clock, in part because it was of year duration and was by no means easy to install; indeed the only place we could find to put it had been on the angle of a high staircase. A further problem was that the case was in three hinged parts, the front door, the main body of the clock containing the movement, and the back board, down which a heavy weight slid.

We duly got out a very tall pair of steps and placed them on the angle of the staircase, alongside the clock, where they seemed to be uncomfortably close to the edge. It was John who volunteered to climb the ladder whilst I had the perilous job of holding it! It is surprising how such a thing steadies one up. Within an hour or so all was well and we could retire thankfully to bed.

The following year one of the other clocks was giving trouble. We should have gone out to Switzerland to sort it out, but were busy at the time and so took advantage of the Swiss clockmaker's offer to attend to the problem for us and gave him the client's name and address. This was to prove a major mistake as the clockmaker was of a very persuasive nature and convinced the client that in future it would be much easier to buy clocks through him.

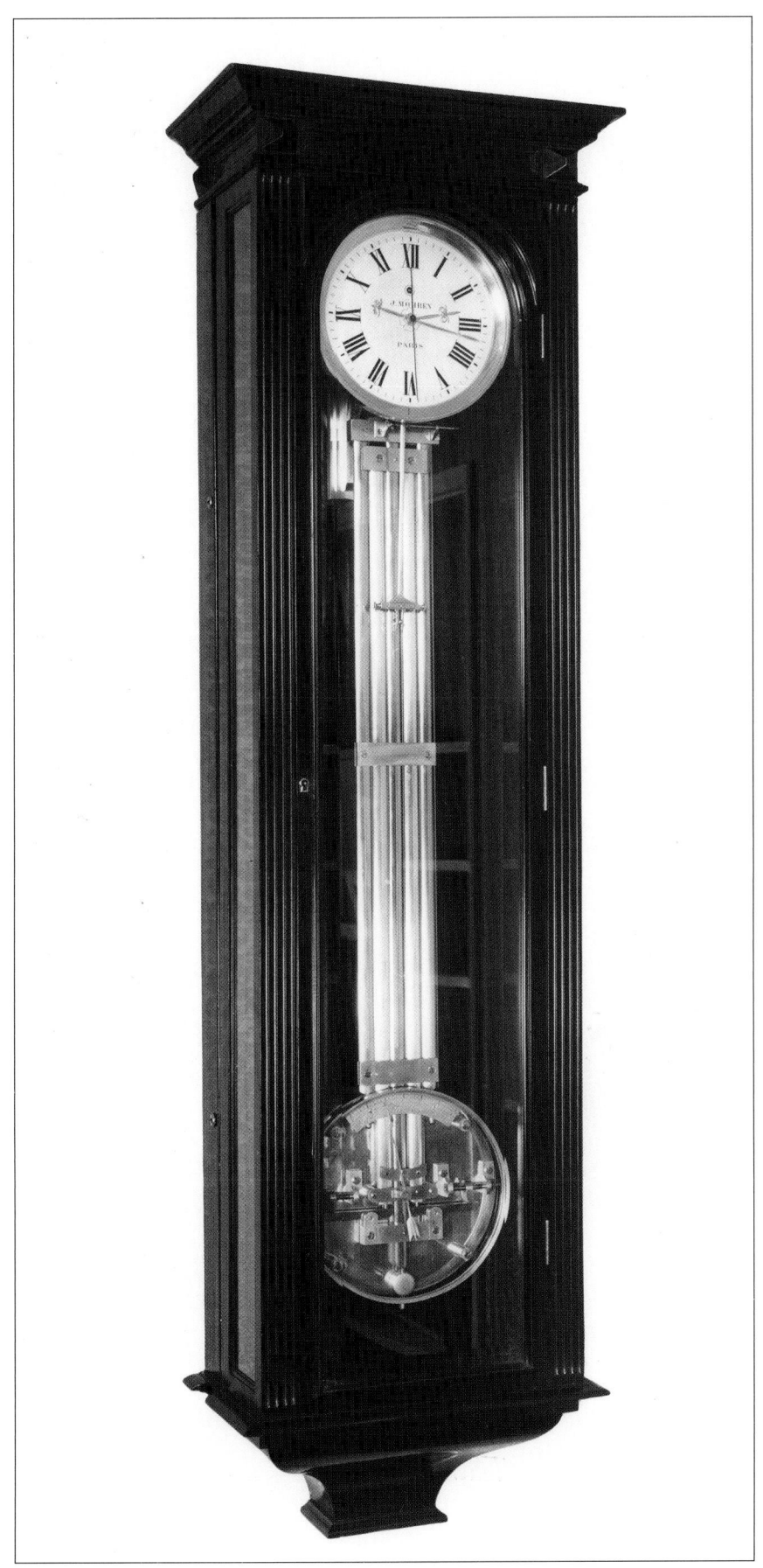

Figure 15. **The massive year-duration wall regulator by Möhren,** which was to give us some anxious moments high up on a wall in Switzerland late one night.

Chapter 8
Monte Carlo & Grimaldi

Monte Carlo

In around 1980 we had the chance of purchasing a business in Monte Carlo. The owner, a Mr Moseley, had a relatively small establishment there in an excellent location. Unfortunately I imagine it was relatively under-funded and thus he dealt in quite inexpensive items, which really wasn't the best thing to do in an area where much of the population was affluent. He did occasionally have fine items through his hands which he had generally acquired from English people who had lived or settled out there. I can remember buying a particularly fine musical clock from him (figure 16) through an intermediary and he also, at one time, had a good Tompion bracket clock.

The reason I believe he wanted to sell the business at this time was primarily because of the poor health of his partner. He felt that she would be more secure under the shelter of the Health Service and I got the impression that he too would like to return to the UK.

The site was a very good one and you could scarcely better the address: No. 1 Buckingham Palace, Monte Carlo. Moreover, I had always had a bit of a love affair with the Principality since we drove on the rally through the best part of some 2000 miles of snow and ice and then descended into Monte Carlo, which was bathed in sunshine and looked almost like paradise. This was in the days before all the development occurred and Bridget Bardot was at the height of her fame with posters of her everywhere.

The first time I went down to the Principality was with an intermediary who had a villa further down the coast in a village a few miles inland. He oscillated between England and France every three months and had by then made the journey over seventy times.

We discussed obvious items such as purchase price, stock, etc. Evidently at that time there were no rates. The main hurdle to be overcome was being approved by Prince Rainier or one of his emissaries. He was quite selective as to whom he allowed to start up in business at that time. There were also strict limits as to how many businesses/ shops of any one type that were allowed, to try and secure a good balance and no undue competition. However, this would not have been a problem in my case as I would be taking over an established business, but I would still have to be approved and take a crash course in French.

The basic concept was that I would spend 2-3 of the winter months out there and possibly at other times as and when necessary, and that someone else would take care of the business for the rest of the year. Here I was lucky in probably having the ideal person to do this. She was a highly skilled clockmaker, had an excellent personality and had spent some two years working in Holland and three in Paris.

I flew home to consider the matter and came back some ten days later to try and make up my mind. One of the main problems at that time was that it was before we had joined the Common Market and the transfer of goods too and from France involved not only time and money but also taxes. It was felt that this would be a serious stumbling block as, if the clocks were not freely interchangeable between the two businesses, then the proposed venture in Monte Carlo would have to be stocked from scratch, and this would not be easy because only relatively high value items would be appropriate. Moreover, we would have to go through the learning curve of what did and did not sell in Monte Carlo. For all these reasons, and others, we decided not to go ahead with the purchase.

One of the big pluses was that good villas were available at relatively modest cost. Owners, who often only came down once or twice a year, were only too happy to have someone who was known to them occupying their property.

At that time, things were always handled there as discretely as possible. I remember the story of an American who bought two apartments where he installed girls to supplement his income and subsequently purchased a property for himself. One evening, two gentlemen arrived at his home and handed him an envelope which, on opening it, he found contained a ticket for the last flight out to America that night. They asked him to pack a suitcase and they would be pleased to entertain him to dinner prior to driving him to the airport. He had no choice, even though he knew he would be losing his properties.

Grimaldi

I had always resisted the lure of having a showroom in the West End, in part due to the high costs involved and also because you were virtually forced into leasing rather than buying a property. A further factor was that I did not want to travel up to London regularly; I had done it in the past but did not enjoy it, and also did not want to neglect the business in Tonbridge which was running very successfully, had plenty of space for cabinet and clockmakers, and also a good showroom.

My opinion changed somewhat when a colleague suggested that we jointly take a lease on a gallery in Royal Arcade (figure 17) off Bond Street. This had the potential advantage that my cost of having a showroom in the West End would be halved and that we could then afford to employ someone else, whom we knew and had confidence in, to run it. I would go up there for one half day a week, which in any case was on the day I went up to London to play squash with a friend and have a meal afterwards, so was of little inconvenience.

I should really have known better! In such a personal world as antiques, unless you are in a very big way of business, you have to be on site for at least much of the time to build up and maintain a level of personal trust and a good relationship with customers. Within two years the business was closed down as there was little chance of it going into profit and the reasonably modest loss was accepted as part of the learning curve. The only disappointment was that the Tax Inspector would not let me offset the loss against the profit on my main business.

Figure 16. **A superb musical bracket clock by Ellicott** which was purchased, through an intermediary, from a dealer in Monte Carlo, whose business, at a later date, we were interested in but did not buy.

Figure 17. **The Grimaldi showroom in Royal Arcade, Bond Street, London.**

Chapter 9
The von Bertele Collection

It was in March 1982 that I went to Vienna to meet Prof. von Bertele who had one of the finest and certainly the most diverse and fascinating collections of clocks in Europe or indeed anywhere. He was an interesting man, graduating in Vienna before the war and subsequently working for the firm of Elsin there. When the conflict was over, he came to England to join the sister company of Nevelin as research manager where he specialised and wrote many articles on mercury and rectifiers. One of his discoveries, with Denne Gabor, was film emission. In 1950 he returned to Vienna where he founded the Institute of Industrial Electronics at the Technical University. By the time he retired in 1973 he had registered some 150 patents.

Prof. von Bertle's main interest in private life was clocks, amassing a substantial collection over the years. He carried out research in many areas of horology; of particular interest being his work on Jost Burgi and the invention of the cross beat escapement; the rolling ball clocks, first devised by Margraf and his survey and articles on Equation clocks. He also fully revised 'The Book of Old Clocks and Watches' by Ernst von Bassermann-Jordan, one of the best books ever written on horology in general, which was first published in German and subsequently translated into English by Alan Lloyd.

The main purpose of the visit to Prof. von Bertele was twofold: (a) To obtain details and photographs for my book on skeleton, mystery, novelty and fantasy clocks, of which he had many good examples, mainly Viennese, and (b) to view his entire collection.

Its strength was in the enormously wide range of the clocks, which I had not seen anywhere else, except possibly in The Time Museum in America, now disbanded. Inevitably there were quite a large number of wall and floorstanding Vienna Regulators including minatures and examples of year duration, but in many ways more interesting were the skeleton, mystery, novelty and fantasy clocks, such as the three train weight driven skeleton clock (figure 18) of extreme delicacy and another supported by two beautifully executed fire gilt dolphins, in which there is no apparent driving force (figure 19).

Figure 18. **An extremely delicate three-train, weight driven, Viennese, skeleton clock.** *Bertele collection*

Figure 19. **A beautiful Viennese mystery clock** with no apparent driving force. *Bertele collection*

Probably the finest was the month duration skeletonised table regulator depicting world time which is reputed to have been made for Francis 1st of Austria by Pechan of Vienna in 1796 (figure 20).

Figure 20. **A most attractive month duration skeletonised table regulator** depicting world time which is reputed to have been made for Francis 1st of Austria by Pechan, Vienna in 1796. The dials, from top to bottom, indicate:

(a) The years marked 1-4, which allows for the leap years
(b) Days of the month and months of the year
(c) Seconds, minutes and hours
(d) A world time dial, with Vienna at the top, showing the time in 48 places by means of a central rotating disc within, which is a rotating lunar disc and in the centre a four sided star marked N, S, E & W. *Bertele collection*

One of the most beautiful clocks was the one by Mathias Ratzenhofer, Vienna, circa 1830, where a ladybird and a butterfly are used to indicate the time (figure 21).

Another fascinating clock was the candle alarm in an engraved gilt case, made in South Germany, circa 1760. It contained a small box of flints, an alarm bell and a candle. To one side is a fusee movement with verge escapement and alarm disc. An arm projecting from this allows the lid to spring open and release a flint which strikes a steel plate causing a spark which lights some tinder and thus the candle that springs into an upright position so as to illuminate the clock.

Figure 21. **A beautiful clock by Mathias Ratzenhofer, Vienna, circa 1830.** The mother of pearl base contains a music box and a fully skeletonised two train quarter striking movement. The hours are indicated by a ladybird moving along a series of Arabic numerals whilst for the minutes a butterfly proceeds over a narrow strip above and every 30 minutes flies back to her start point. *Bertele collection*

The most important clock was the one by Nicholas Radeloff, circa 1660, (figures 22 a & b) which, by an odd coincidence, had previously been owned by a customer and friend of ours. It was driven by rolling balls and employed a cross beat escapement. The latter, invented by Jost Burgi, was the last attempt to make an accurate escapement prior to the invention of the anchor in 1657. All records of it had been lost, although reference had been found to a 'Precision Escapement' and it was only in the 1950s when the rock crystal clock in Vienna was investigated that it was realised that the reference was actually to a refined form of verge escapement with Foliot, now known as the cross-beat. It was not to be too long after this before three other clocks by Radeloff were rediscovered in Rosenborg Castle in Denmark, and all had their original cross-beat escapements. The basic principle of the cross-beat is the use of a single escape wheel but two separate pallets, each of which is carried by its own arbor; these being connected by two pinions. Attached to the ends of the arbors are two decorative arms which constantly cross and recross as the clock 'beats'; a fascinating sight.

Figures 22 a, b. **The Radelof rolling ball clock** with cross beat escapement, circa 1660. The balls which drive the clock may be seen descending down a spiral track and as they do so pressing on a vertical bar and thus powering the clock. The basic principle of the cross beat is the use of a single escape wheel but two separate pallets, each of which is carried by its own arbor, these being interlinked by two pinions so that as the clock 'beats' the arms attached to the ends of the arbors cross and recross, as in figure 23. *Bertele collection*

Besides the Radeloff, there was a further small clock with cross-beat escapement in the collection, signed Franciscus Schwartz in Bruessel (figure 23).

Figure 23. **Franciscus Schwartz in Brussels, circa 1660**. A small clock incorporating a cross-beat escapement. *Bertele collection*

The earliest and most complex clock in the collection was the fine astronomical table clock attributed to Jeremias Metzger. Its complexity is such that it would not be practical to give a full description of it here (figure 24). Suffice it to say that the four sides of the clock have, in all, ten dials, giving much astronomical and astrological information. The very complex iron movements made in the second half of the 16th century, must have been extremely expensive to make, reflecting the great wealth of the country at that time.

Figure 24. **A fine and complex astronomical clock** attributed to Jeremias Metzger, circa 1575. This clock was made in an era of great wealth. The movement has brass plates and pillars, and iron wheels and pinions. It has going and quarter hour striking trains with fusee and balance.

The numerous dials are too complex to describe here. Suffice it to say that the front dial has a narrow double 12-hour chapter ring, a central astrolabe with the zodiacal signs, tympanum, dragon, sun and moon hands, a diagram of aspects and the phases of the moon. There are also dials to the back and either side. *Bertele collection*

Another fascinating clock, made a little later, was the pillar clock by Joachim Oberkircher of Vienna (figure 25), which has two dials, one astronomical and the other astrological.

Figures 25 a, b. **A rare Viennese pillar clock** with astronomical and astrological dials, circa 1680. The astronomical dial is, in effect, a rotating year calendar. The outer two rings show the day of the week and the day of the month. Inside these are some of the saint's days. The other rings show the month with its number of days, the signs of the zodiac with their symbol and picture, the hours of daylight and the times of sunrise and sunset.

The astrological dial indicates 2-12 hours in roman numerals, quarter hours and 1-24 for the astrological hours which are 12 hours out of phase with mean time. The seven rings towards the centre of the dial represent the days of the week with their planetary dieties. With this information you can establish the ruling planets for a particular hour and decide whether you want to conclude a deal, go on a journey or even get married! Bertele collection.

A rare clock was the one by Father Philip Hahn of Echterdingen, (figure 26) circa 1781, with a Copernican celestial sphere of enamel painted on copper and above this a small globe representing the moon.

Figure 26. **A rare clock by Father Philip Hahn of Echterdingen, circa 1781.** The double, 12-hour dial has subsidiary dials for seconds and minutes. Above it is a finely executed rotating celestial sphere of enamel painted on copper and above this again a small rotating globe representing the moon. *Bertele collection*

Switzerland

Clocks from Switzerland were mainly represented by the eminent maker Jaquet-Droz, who, unfortunately, seldom signed his clocks.

The first of these was a seven tune organ clock (one of two) employing 15 pipes to play seven different tunes. It also had grande sonnerie striking (figure 27).

Figure 27. **A seven-tune organ clock** (one of two) with ebonised case and ornate frets and mirrors. It employs 15 pipes and plays seven tunes. It also has grande sonnerie striking. Below the main convex enamelled dial is the maker's plaque 'Jaquet Droz a la Chaux de fonds', circa 1780. *Bertele collection*

The second (figures 28 a & b) was a double-dialled clock by the same maker, one to tell the time during the day and the other at night.

Figures 28 a, b. **Jaquet Droz day and night clock**, originally with turntable base so that the correct dial was always facing front. The conventional 12-hour convex enamelled dial has a picture below it of a courting couple. At night a small oil lamp would be placed inside the clock and the smoke allowed to go out through the funnel above. The numerals are perforated in the engraved and gilded dial plate so that they can be seen illuminated at night. The pendulum hangs in front of the day dial to prevent it casting a shadow at night. *Bertele collection* (Above and right)

France

France at probably its finest period of clockmaking, was represented by, amongst others, a fine spring driven table regulator by Robin, with remontoire, which was presented by Louis XVI to the Governor of St Pierre et Miquelon (Quebec). Janvier was represented by three clocks; a weight driven table regulator (figure 29), and another complete with travelling case, which is believed to have been designed to assess the height of mountains. In the third clock by Janvier, of year duration, the movement was incorporated in the pendulum bob.

Also in the collection were some early tortoiseshell religieuse clocks and a couple of French organ clocks.

Figure 29. **Antide Janvier.** A weight-driven table regulator with calendar-work and moon phases, dated 1780. *Bertele collection*

England

English late 17th or early 18th century bracket clocks in the collection included examples of the work of Quare (two); Fromanteel; Fromanteel & Clarke & Peter Garon. A particularly interesting clock by Quare and Horseman, known as the Cinderella clock (figures 30 a & b), is believed to have had the movement fitted to its case in Paris, where it would have been manufactured.

A later, but rare clock, was the month duration longcase regulator by Reid & Auld, that had originally been fitted with spring pallets, which were reinstated by von Bertele.

The list is far from complete but will give some indication of the breadth of the collection, which, scarcely surprisingly, included many fine Viennese wall, floor-standing, mystery, novelty and fantasy clocks.

While we were in Vienna, we visited some other collectors and also dealers, and had already made appointments to visit the two major museums which had extensive collections of clocks.

The curator of the Sobek collection at the Geymuller Schlössl just outside Vienna was particularly helpful, opening up the museum to me one cold winter's day and giving me every assistance in examining the excellent Viennese clocks in their possession. We also visited the Vienna Clock Museum to examine their fine and important clocks.

The Death of Professor von Bertele

It was in 1984 that I received a phone call from a school friend of mine, who had married the eldest daughter of Prof. von Bertele, informing me that Prof. von Bertele had died and that his wife had inherited the clocks. He asked if I could come out to Vienna to advise on them and this I was pleased to do. At that time I had the opportunity to meet the other members of the family, other than Prof. von Bertele's wife who had died a few years earlier.

The initial task was to make a catalogue of the collection, together with polaroid photographs for identification and then assess the value of each of them, by no means an easy task because of the range and complexity of the clocks; however, in due course provisional prices were applied to nearly all of them, in a few instances assisted by some notes which Prof. von Bertele left behind.

It was decided at this stage to divide the clocks into three groups:

(a) Those that the family wished to retain.

(b) The clocks that it was decided should be disposed of locally.

(c) Some that had an international appeal and it was felt would be best brought back to England to be sold. To do this, we had to get approval, which involved the Government's Office for the Protection of Austrian Heritage; the latter being advised by the Director of the Vienna Clock Museum. Eventually this was forthcoming.

To my surprise, the first person to come to the house to see the clocks for sale immediately enquired about a clock I thought little of and indeed had not even valued. It basically consisted of a rectangular wooden base on which rested a fully glazed case formed from angled brass. The dial was of silvered brass and the weight driven single train movement was of a type which was being mass produced in the first part of the 20th century, as was the seconds beating pendulum.

To me, judged by its age and quality, it was only worth a few hundred pounds; however, I hesitated to say this, in part because of the obvious enthusiasm of the visitor and also because of my equally obvious lack of appreciation. I thus replied that we had not come to a decision on the price of the clock at this stage, whereupon he promptly, to my amazement, offered a very substantial sum which I said we would consider. In fact, the clock finally sold for a much higher price. It turned out that it had been designed by Adolf Loos, the renowned Austrian Art Deco architect and designer. A year later when I returned to Vienna, I saw it taking pride of place in an exhibition of his work.

It was fairly early on in the transaction that we were visited by a well known Austrian dealer and collector who said that he was interested in buying the entire collection and asked me to give him an inventory, with prices, for all the clocks.

By this time I had priced all those that were available for sale with the exception of the Nicholas Radeloff, and here we were relying on the notes of Prof. von Bertele who said that he had been offered a very substantial sum for it by Seth Attwood of The Time Museum some years ago when he had come to see the collection and thus the figure we used in the inventory was based on this.

It turned out that the Austrian collector who approached us was acting on behalf of an important Swiss collector who, with his advisors, felt that the price for the Radeloff was far too high, particularly as The Time Museum refused to confirm that any offer had been made to Prof. von Bertele, and thus our offer was rejected. In favour of the clock was its extreme rarity; only three other similar Radeloffs' existed, all in Denmark, and these were very unlikely to ever come on the market. However, all these were in substantially original condition whereas von Bertele had had to carry out very extensive restoration to his example, including the reinstatement of the escapement.

We then proceeded with the sale of the clocks in Vienna and over the next six months homes were found for virtually all of them.

By this time, approval had been granted for the export of the remaining clocks to England and this was arranged. We eventually bought two of them and others were included in an exhibition we had. Finally, they were all sold except the Radeloff, which I am pleased to say subsequently reached the ideal home when it was bought for a castle in Schleswig, thanks to a kind benefactor. A fitting finale was that Prof. von Bertele's daughter who inherited the clocks, and her husband, saw the Radeloff after it was installed in its new home, close to where Nicholas Radeloff had been born.

Figures 30 a, b. **Quare and Horseman, London, No. 214, circa 1725.** The case of this clock, which is veneered in tortoiseshell and decorated with delicate brass inlay, is thought to have been made in Paris where the movement was fitted to it. It chimes the quarters on four bells and has a superbly engraved backplate. The dial is finely executed. *Bertele collection.* (Above and right)

Chapter 10
Horological Publications, Exhibitions, Catalogues & Fairs

It was almost inevitable that having carried out research in the dental field that I should head in the same direction with clocks.

Books

Figure 31. **The first two books we were to write on Horology:** *Skeleton Clocks,* **Britain 1800-1914**, (right) published by The Antique Collectors Club, and *Continental and American Skeleton Clocks*, which was produced by Schiffer Publishing in the USA, some two years later.

British, Continental and American Skeleton Clocks

The first area I became interested in was skeleton clocks. These are fascinating because they have no case, just a protective glass dome, and as much of the movement as possible is cut away, in a decorative style, so as to display exactly how it works; moreover the workmanship is usually of a much higher standard than that usually encountered and sometimes of greater complexity.

All the clocks we bought or sold, even from quite early days, were carefully documented and photographed, initially by a professional photographer and later by myself, thus we already had pictures and descriptions of quite a lot of skeleton clocks; however, many more were needed if a book was to be published on the subject and at that time little was available from the auction houses as a lot of the clocks were not illustrated in their catalogues and the pictures of those that were, were often inadequate.

A similar situation applied with the museums, which held very few skeleton clocks and the number in private hands was also small, there being only one major collector in the UK; all the important ones being in America. There was thus no alternative, if I were to write the book, than to contact them and organise a tour. By this time I had acquired a Hasselblad camera, probably the best there was available at that time, complete with a set of lenses and interchangeable backs so that I could take black and white, colour negative and colour transparencies without having to change the film or disturb the camera in any way. This was important because at that time colour printing was expensive and the number of colour pictures you were permitted to use in a book was strictly limited. A friend of mine was allowed just eight in a book of some 550 pages.

If I was to take my pictures in America I also needed floodlights with their stands and umbrellas, and couldn't use those I had as they were for 230 volt whereas in America the supply was 110 volt. The last thing I needed was a good background material.

All of the above required quite a large case to accommodate them and thus I made do with an overnight bag for my personal use. I had not realised that American customs would be so strict about the amount of photographic equipment I was taking in; evidently I should have had a carnet of some sort, but in the end they let me through.

I started off in New York where I met one or two dealers and collectors who were most hospitable. This was my first time in the States and I found it very interesting. From there I went to the Time Museum, where Seth Atwood was already starting to amass a fine collection and then on to Seattle to see someone who had built up an impressive range of clocks, including many skeleton and also mystery clocks. He came to England regularly and had many friends in the horological world over here. We photographed all his skeleton and mystery

clocks as I had at that time hoped to include the latter in my book, but in the end abandoned this idea as it would have made the book far too long; however, these pictures eventually came into their own when I wrote a book on Mystery, Novelty and Fantasy clocks. I was also introduced to a friend of his who had some interesting American skeleton clocks.

From there I flew down to Los Angeles, getting there around 6.00 pm and feeling rather tired. I suggested that I set up and photograph a few clocks that evening, but he had other ideas and said that as we could take pictures of his clocks any time, we should drive down the coast to see the clocks of a friend, some of which were very interesting. We arrived around eight o'clock and for the first time I experienced an example of American enthusiasm. The telephone started ringing and then clocks arriving until maybe 12 that night and quite a party developed. I arranged to have lunch the next day with someone who ran a crematorium where he kept his collection, mostly mystery, novelty and fantasy clocks. Six of us were due to have lunch together, but in the end maybe twenty turned up.

In the afternoon we went to see the clocks, an interesting collection and as I was leaving he opened a large cupboard full of his latest line, which he said was a great success; commemorative mugs which could be painted up with the deceased's name etc at very short notice!

I hired a car in Los Angeles and drove down to San Diego, calling in at an interesting collector/dealer on the way who, in particular, had one or two clocks by James Condliff, probably the finest skeleton clock-maker in the UK. The clocks in San Diego proved to be fine also and I have very pleasant memories of the clam chowder and pacific prawns.

My last port of call before flying home, was to visit a serious collector in Washington who had many fine skeleton clocks, all of which were most interesting, and one or two almost unique. These were a valuable addition for the book; however, I had hoped at this stage to do a little business, either buying or selling, to help defray some of the cost of the trip, but it was not to be.

I had an uneventful trip home with the inevitable difficulty with customs as far as the photographic equipment was concerned and then I anxiously awaited the processing of the films. Fortunately, all was in order; the few failures which occurred being of no consequence.

The next overseas trip was to the Conservatoire National Des Arts et Metiers in Paris, which had many unusual and fine clocks. I realised that I could not take any photographs there but looked at all those on display and made notes, both about the clocks and also the photographs I would require. One of the most fascinating had square wheels.

I had an introduction to the museum curator, Madam Catherine Cardinal, who kindly gave me free access to their fine collection and agreed to look through the photographs they had and then arrange for the others which were needed to be taken. This was at the end of October, but, unfortunately, by

January she had left for pastures new before the photography had been carried out. I was then back to the beginning as the new curator refused to allow the cabinets to be opened so that the clocks could be photographed. The outcome was that in the end I received some but by no means all of the pictures required.

The Gold and Silver Museum in the charming little town of Schoonhöven in Holland, which had a fine collection of skeleton clocks, mainly by the eminent maker Verneuil, were particularly helpful. They suggested I come on a day when the museum was closed and when I arrived just opened up their cabinets and left me to it.

My last port of call before I sat down to complete the research on the book and then write it was Vienna, the home of so much fine clock making, where Professor Hans von Bertele had a very fine collection of clocks, including many unusual skeletons which he supplied me with pictures of. He also introduced me to other collectors and museums such as the Sobek Collection at the Geymuller Schlössl and the Vienna Clock Museum.

The stage had now been reached where I had to contact museums, dealers, collectors etc, and check in as many books as I could to gain all the information which I needed about the clocks and their makers. It was then that everything started to fall into place and I could sit down and write the book.

The manuscript was submitted to the Antique Collectors Club in 1986, when, because of the size of it, it was decided to split it into two: *British Skeleton Clocks* (figure 31), which was published the following year, and *Continental and American Skeleton Clocks* (figure 31), which was contracted to follow six months later, but this did not happen. Twelve, eighteen and then twenty-four months went by and it was at this stage that Schiffer Publishing in America approached me to do a book on longcase clocks. I mentioned my difficulties with the second part of skeleton clocks and they agreed, if I let them have the manuscript, to have it published within six months, and this they did. In return, I let them have a manuscript on *British Longcase Clocks* (figure 32), which was not an in-depth study of the subject but largely written to give readers some idea of all the different types available. This was published in 1990.

To coincide with the publication of our first book on skeleton clocks, we collected together over fifty examples, many of them rare, with a variety of escapements, frames, strikework and originating from various different countries. A lot of them showed great ingenuity, one employing a rolling ball, another having a revolving escapement (tourbillon) and a third being made entirely of ivory. Others represented famous buildings such as St Paul's, Westminster Abbey and Brighton Pavilion. This was the first time that such an exhibition had been held and proved to be a great success.

Carriage Clocks

It was in 1974 that Charles Allix and Peter Bonnert's excellent book on carriage clocks was published. Much time and many trips to France were given over to researching the subject and the result was a full history of the origins and development of the carriage clock, and a list with all the known details of the makers, together with their marks, which was to prove invaluable to collectors and dealers in the years to come. Unfortunately, it had been published in an era when colour reproduction was very expensive and thus it was produced almost entirely in black and white. This was a shame as the best carriage clocks with their beautiful porcelain and limoges enamel panels, fine champlevé enamel and engraving, to name but some of their various forms of decoration, were objects of real beauty.

To overcome this problem, we decided to do a book which was in many ways complimentary to Allix and Bonnert, leaving out much of the history and the list of makers, and concentrating on their aesthetic appeal, all the different forms of decoration used, the methods of manufacture, and some of their mechanical complexities, which we had been able to record, thanks to the Hasselblad camera.

As we had had many hundreds of fine carriage clocks through our hands over the years, the material for the book was not a problem, particularly as we received unstinting support from museums, auction houses, other dealers and collectors.

It was in 1993 that this book was published by Schiffer in America.

Mystery, Novelty & Fantasy Clocks

This book, which was published in 1999, was something of a personal indulgence, loving as I did the amazing ingenuity of some clockmakers, many of which were French. A typical example is Robert Houdin, France's most famous magician and after whom Houdini the escapologist took his name. He produced a series of clocks of varying complexity with clear glass dials in which there was no apparent connection between the movement and the hands, and yet they went round. Another, made by his uncle, featured a seated magician who mysteriously changed the objects such as dice, below cups in his hands.

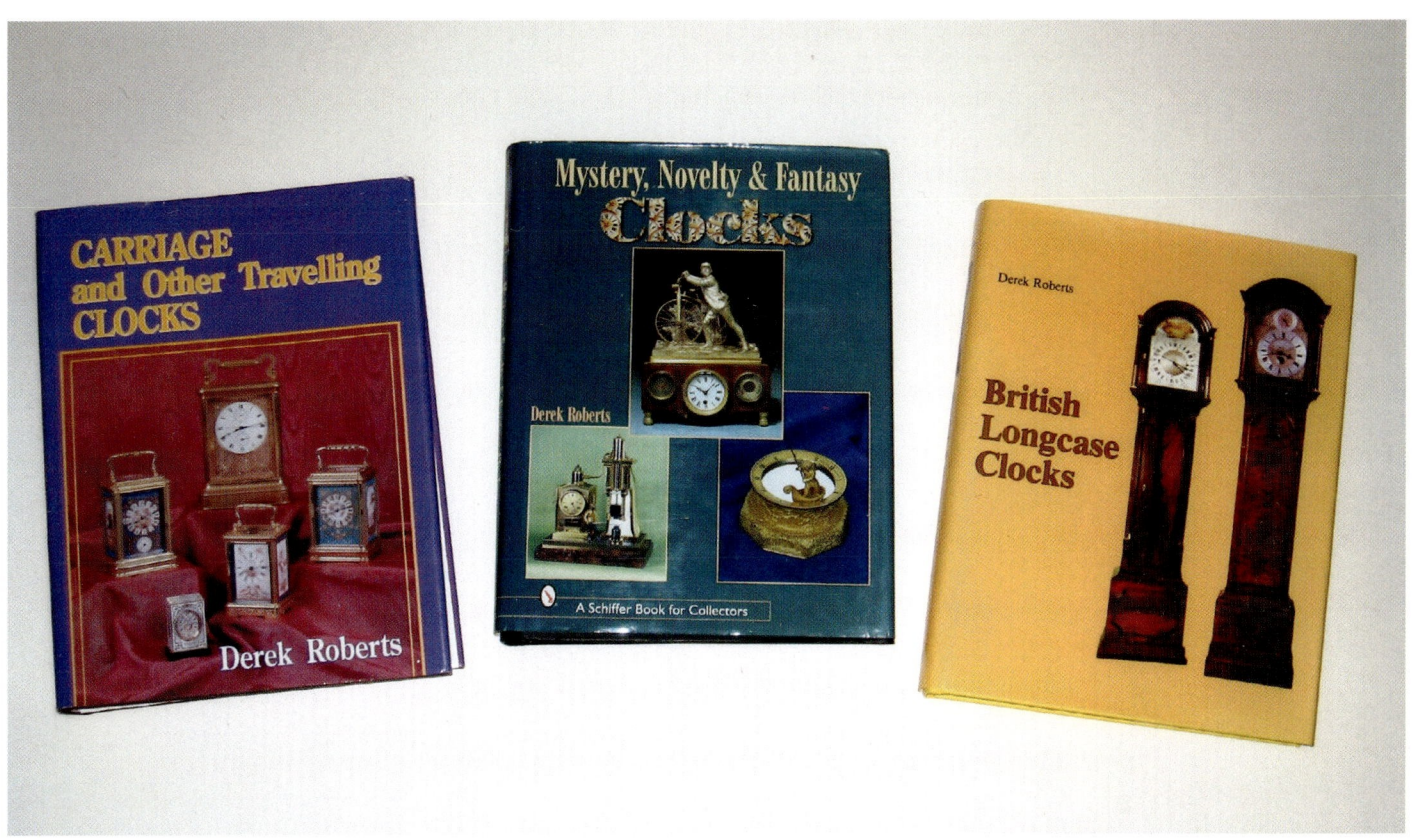

Figure 32. **The books** *Carriage and Other Travelling Clocks;* *Mystery, Novelty & Fantasy Clocks;* **and** *British Longcase Clocks,* **published by Schiffer Publishing.** *British Longcas Clocks* was not an in-depth study of the subject, but rather written to explain all the different types produced and the changes in their design over the centuries.

Carriage and Other Travelling Clocks was conceived to illustrate, mainly in colour, all the different case styles produced, the numerous ways, such as porcelain panels and enamelling, engraving etc, in which they were decorated, and their technical features. Charles Allix and Peter Bonnert had already covered their early history and development and produced a list of the makers.

Mystery, Novelty & Fantasy Clocks was something of a self-indulgence, as I was fascinated by the ingenuity and skill of the clockmakers and many of the more highly individual clocks they had produced.

Guilmet designed a clock which featured a pendulum, suspended from the outstretched hand of a statue, which had no apparent connection to the clock and yet controlled its timekeeping (figure 33), and indeed the statue could be lifted off the clock to show that they were not linked in any way. Other clocks were made which were either driven or regulated by rolling balls.

Further examples of the clockmaker's skill were those mimicking a rower, a helmsman, a train, a steam hammer, a steam pump, a windmill and many other objects. Some had pendulums which had a circular, as opposed to a to-and-fro motion whilst still others had birds who sang a song. The list is almost endless.

Figure 33. **A mystery clock by Guilmet** in which the pendulum has no apparent connection to the movement and yet controls it; indeed the statue, complete with pendulum, can be lifted off the clock.

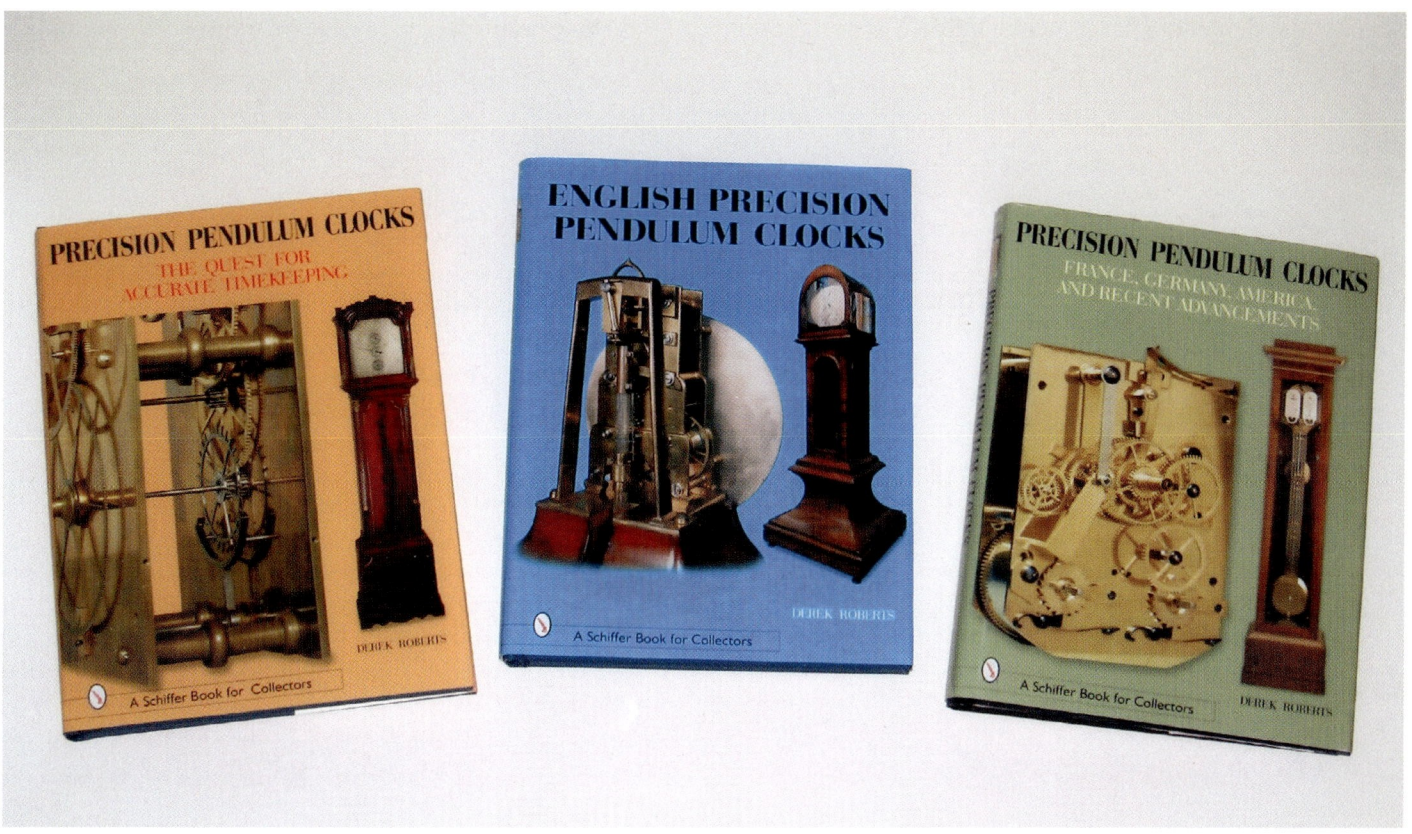

Figure 34. *Precision Pendulum Clocks* was conceived as one book in three volumes, but the publishers decided to publish it as three separate books: (1) *Precision Pendulum Clocks, The Quest for Accurate Timekeeping.* (2) *English Precision Pendulum Clocks.* (3) *Precision Pendulum Clocks, France, Germany, America and Recent Advancements.*

Precision Pendulum Clocks (or regulators)

The quest to record time accurately has been the principal aim of clockmakers from 1657 onwards when the pendulum had first been applied to clocks and even before that efforts had been made to improve their timekeeping. This was essential if progress was to be made in astronomy, cartography and a multitude of other areas and even to regulate our lives by.

Surprisingly, although various aspects of this quest have appeared in print over the centuries, no-one had written a book on the subject, bringing all the various aspects together, until Klaus Erbrich's book *Präzisionspendeluhren* was published by Callwey in Germany in 1978. It had been hoped that an English edition would be produced, but this was not to be.

We supplied many illustrations for his book and were pleased to see it published, but did not feel it really covered the subject in the manner and depth which was required, and so we continued to collect suitable material and photographs.

Some years later, a consortium of four horologists in this country, two of whom had already written books, decided to write one on precision pendulum clocks, and so we passed all our material over to them. Sadly after four or five years they decided not to proceed and so we received all our photographs back again and continued to gather up all the available material.

It was to be several years later that a friend of ours decided to write the book but, probably wisely, he abandoned the project some six months later.

When I reached 65 I realised that if the story of the quest for accurate timekeeping was ever to be told, I would have to start it then. Knowing that it would absorb an enormous amount of time, despite the material already collected, I decided to cut my attendance at the business down to two days a week, which I thought it would probably stand, and devote the rest of my time to writing, research and photography.

The latter proved to be much more of an uphill struggle than I had anticipated, primarily because many of the important clocks, such as those by Harrison, had never been photographed adequately or in enough detail to illustrate their technical features. Jonathan Betts of the National Maritime Museum was particularly helpful in this respect, enabling me to obtain or take photographs at his museum and also at Belmont. I was also able to take pictures of the Harrison's owned by the Clockmakers Company when they were on loan to Greenwich.

Gradually the book gathered momentum and photographs and information came in from many different sources. Dieter Riefler allowed me to use material taken from his book on

Riefler, Präzisions Pendeluhren von 1890-1965, and Hans-Jochen Kummer gave me similar co-operation with his book on Strasse and Rohde as did Herbert Dittrich who contributed the section on their precision clocks.

The actual writing of the book, which ran to three volumes, took around 3,500 hours, excluding all the proof reading, but by the end of 2001, when I had reached 70, the massive manuscript went off to the publishers.

The decision to produce the book in three separate volumes (figure 34) was a joint one and they allowed me to decide on the way it should be split up. The only decision which disappointed me was to publish the three volumes separately, ie with a gap of around six months between each of them; however, this was a commercial decision which I had to go along with, particularly as they had agreed to publish it in its entirety without any reductions or omissions and include all the colour photography. The decision to separate the publication dates had the advantage, from my point of view, that it reduced the pressure of proof reading. The major disadvantage was that it adversely affected all the cross-referencing which had been so carefully worked out, as they insisted that each book should start with page 1 and chapter 1, thus one has, for instance, three page 25s and three chapter 3s, something I was strongly opposed to. The figure numbers were kept running consecutively with the references but, for instance in Chapter 8 of *English Precision Pendulum Clocks*, the figures start at 18, which leads to further confusion.

Paul Archard

It was at this stage that I felt that my debt to horology, which had given me so much pleasure, was finally fulfilled and I decided to give up the business, particularly as my staff appeared to be looking at me with increasingly worried eyes and wondering how much longer I could go on and how secure their futures were. Most of them had been with us for upwards of 25 years.

I was extremely lucky in finding in Paul Archard, the ideal person to take over the business, lock, stock and barrel. He lived locally – I had known him for maybe thirty years, although not closely. I had bought some clocks off him which he had restored in his early years. He had pursued a successful career in the city and during this period had bought a few clocks off us and more elsewhere, and built up a fine collection. Throughout he had a keen interest in horology and had even made four regulators.

He had retired from the city early, and maybe when I approached him was at a loose end and wanted another interest. When the transaction was completed, the staff breathed a sigh of relief as he was the best part of 20 years younger than me. I am delighted to say, that, despite difficult times, all has gone well.

Exhibitions, Catalogues and Fairs

In our early days, as mentioned earlier, we did a limited number of fairs, usually in Kent but occasionally straying into Surrey and Sussex. These were virtually all of short duration, maybe 1, 2 or 4 days, but generally running over a weekend.

These were usually fun to do; it was easy to take the stock to the fair and set it up, using our own transport and as they were generally held in some of the more prestigious hotels such as the Spa at Tunbridge Wells, there was a pleasant atmosphere with refreshments always available. Because of the relatively low cost, there were no great financial implications and we generally ended up with a reasonable profit and with a little luck enticed some of the customers back to our showrooms.

It was in January 1974 that we gained membership of the British Antique Dealers Association, the most important body in the world of antiques in this country and at that stage we felt we should participate in some of the London Fairs, the first one of which, if I remember correctly, was Kensington.

It was in October 1983 that we exhibited at the Burlington House Fair (figure 35), a prestigious event in an excellent setting and there we had the privilege of being introduced by Kenneth Snoman to the Queen Mother (figure 36). We found her to be a charming lady who had the knack of almost instantaneously putting you at your ease. She had a genuine interest and enthusiasm for clocks, particularly those which were quarter chiming or musical. I explained that I had three which would play her a tune if she had the time to stay on the stand for a few minutes longer. This she did and was delighted to hear them playing. She then shot off, almost leaving her retinue behind. Her equerry had a chat with me afterwards. He said that every morning he had to make certain that the four clocks where she took her breakfast were all synchronised and exactly on time.

The only slight downside to Burlington was that it was a little dominated by the picture dealers. We made good contacts there and did some useful business. We repeated our attendance at the fair in the following two years. At one of them I met Prince Charles and Lady Diana, but he had none of the enthusiasm of his grandmother. Shortly after this the Fair was discontinued. I was then offered a place at the Grosvenor House Fair but foolishly, from a financial point of view, turned it down and one of my fellow clock dealers was given the stand.

The only other fair we exhibited at after Burlington, which I have fond memories of, was one of those organised by the British Antique Dealers Association. It was excellently run, had a very pleasant atmosphere and a good restaurant, but was to be the last I attended. I just wasn't a fair man and had too many other commitments.

It was to be some three years after becoming a member of the BADA that I was kindly introduced by Mike Baker, a clockmaker who had recently returned from Rhodesia as it was then, to Reginald Beloe and it was he who put my name forward to become a member of the Worshipful Company of Clockmakers, which I felt highly privileged to join, being elevated to the Livery the following year.

The Worshipful Company of Clockmakers was formed in 1631, a comparatively late date for a trading guild; however, up until that time, the relatively small number of clocks that had been made in this country was produced by blacksmiths.

The earliest of the Trading Guilds is that of the Weavers, which was granted by Henry II in 1184. The system of apprenticeships became general at the beginning of the 13th century and the test of good workmanship, ie the production of a 'Masterpiece', which had to satisfy the Master and Court of the company before he was admitted, was adopted some two years later.

The basic functions of the companies was to maintain standards, restrict unfair competition and support their members. It was in the reign of Edward I that the Guilds adopted a distinguishing dress which became known as the 'Livery', hence the name of Liverymen.

It was undoubtedly the formation of the Clockmakers Company, together with the keen interest in the sciences at that time, which enabled British Clockmakers to forge forward and become the leaders in their field in Europe well before the 17th century was out.

To join a company which had such a celebrated history was, I felt and indeed still do feel, both a great privilege and pleasure; moreover, the company still have today a surprisingly high number of members or Liverymen who are active in the world of horology.

I have so far not exercised my right to drive sheep over London Bridge, although I believe someone did so last year, with the help of the police!

Catalogues

The first catalogue we issued, in July 1978, running to 47 pages, was produced to accompany our initial exhibition on Precision Pendulum Clocks and amongst others, featured the wall regulators made by Martin & Roberts.

A much more extensive exhibition of Precision Clocks took place in June 1986 and included many important clocks such as early tank and wall regulators by Riefler (figures 59 and 60), one of which had been with the factory for many years. There was also a Tompion sidereal and mean time regulator (on loan), the only one known, some spectacular regulators by Frodsham (figure 58 AB), and examples of the work of Reid & Auld, Ellicott, Arnold & Brock, amongst others.

Figure 35. **Meeting the Queen Mother,** a clock enthusiast, at the Burlington House Fair.

Figure 36. **Our stand at one of the Burlington House Fairs.**

It was at this time also (June 1986) that we started issuing regular catalogues (figure 37), published on a quarterly basis, with the odd omissions and these were continued until the winter of 1989 when the recession slowed down sales and they became, for a while, uneconomic, although in the past we were achieving sales rates of 50-75%.

In 1987, in part because of our handling of the Bertele collection, we accumulated a considerable number of very rare clocks, and so decided to put them in an exhibition titled Amazing Clocks. The catalogue accompanying it was a fascinating one, running to 90 pages (figure 37).

By 1993 we had resumed our regular catalogues again, but this time on an annual basis and they were always accompanied by an exhibition. This was continued until we sold the business in May 2003 and I am pleased to say that our successor keeps up the tradition and indeed now holds two exhibitions a year

The Website

It was around 1999 that one of the staff, Clive Collins, came to us and asked if we would let him set up a website for the business. We had been approached by one or two professionals in this field in the past, but I had not been particularly impressed by their offerings and the fees seemed very high, so had rejected them. I felt that we had very little to lose in accepting his offer, particularly as he was a very keen member of staff who had been with us over 25 years.

In the event, the website he set up became an invaluable tool for the business and far better and easier to use than many which had been set up professionally. Its main advantages were and still are:

(a) Because space is relatively unlimited and we always had good, usually multiple photographs of all our stock and detailed descriptions of them, clients could get an excellent idea of the pieces being offered to them; far better, for instance, than in an advertisement.

(b) Once someone had seen our stock and been able to appreciate its originality and the care which had been given to the way in which it was restored, they could keep up-to-date with it by referring to our website and should something appeal to them, they could always phone up and discuss it.

Figure 37. **Examples of catalogues** produced by us.

Chapter 11

The Staff

Staff are an integral and very important part of any business, be it only one or a hundred people, and it is essential that when they come in contact with customers that they behave in a friendly and helpful manner. By and large we have been very lucky with those who have worked for us and have had few problems. Those that have occurred have generally been with the younger members of the team. Taking on young girls who, when interviewed, said they had no intention of having a baby but surprisingly two months later were six months pregnant, was one problem encountered; another was the emotional trauma of changing relationships. In one instance, a girl joined us who had left her husband but was not yet divorced and became enamoured with a married man. The problem was not with the wife but the other girlfriend he had.

It did not take too long to realise that the ideal, for a small and very personal business such as ours, was to employ someone of reasonably mature years who no longer wanted to start or add to their family, or change relationships and, with a little luck, would stay with you for many years and become part of the team.

Greg Dallimore

When we started we had just one part-time employee, a retired tea planter whom we had inherited with the business. His loyalty was unquestioned and we could put our complete trust in him. When we went away he would come and live in our home, above and behind the showroom, and would always cover for us if we went out for the day.

He related to customers well, although he had a little difficulty with the younger generation and the casual dress styles which were coming in at that time. One of his phrases, which I think is still valid today, is that 'you have to introduce the customer to the clocks they might be interested in', you know them much better than they do. Valerie and I often went out together on a buying trip on a Saturday and on returning, before coming in, would look through the shop window and count up the sold tickets. On one occasion, there were eight longcase clocks sold and on entering the showroom saw that there were still three people there actively buying. Greg Dallimore was worried about the level of the stock and asked how many more he should let them have. I said it was not a problem as at that time there was still so much available that it didn't matter. He sold thirteen!

Sadly, at the age of 76, he was hit by a car at a dangerous crossing and never fully recovered from his injuries, dying a few years later.

Rosemary Freeman

Until VAT was introduced, we could cope with the bookwork fairly well, but after this, needed help, particularly as the business was expanding quite rapidly, and it was at this stage that Rosemary Freeman appeared on the scene on a part-time basis. She had two youngsters and another was to follow on within a short time, but she seldom allowed this to interfere with her work and it is Rosemary whom I have to thank for making my various publications possible, which, particularly in the early days, was a demanding task, bearing in mind that every time the text was changed in any way at all, at least a page or even a whole chapter had to be typed out again, which probably meant, realistically, that the entire manuscript was typed out at least three times. Today you make any changes on the word processor and it sorts out everything else for you automatically.

Rosemary left us in 1987 to take on a full-time job with a firm of accountants, but we were delighted to welcome her back in March 1998, when she proved invaluable in processing, if that is the right word, my last three publications covering 'The Quest for Accurate Timekeeping'. She is still working with Derek Roberts Antiques today, some five years after I passed the business over to Paul Archard.

Crutch Brothers

At this time, the cabinet makers, Easdens of Chislehurst, whom I largely relied on, had undergone a change when the father died and the son took over. He had a reluctance to let me speak to the craftsmen who would be doing the job, which made things very difficult for me, particularly as he had nowhere near the depth of knowledge of his father and I was thus looking around for someone else.

About 100 yards away from the business were the workshops of Crutch Brothers who were primarily involved with home furnishings, such as curtains, carpets and cabinet work. I introduced myself to them and asked them to do some cabinet work for me. The employee who did this for them was Colin Buckwell, a gifted craftsman in his 20s. It was only maybe a year later in June 1978 that Crutch Brothers, whose shop was in Tunbridge Wells, got into financial difficulties and I bought them out, largely to secure the workshops, which were quite extensive, and the services of their cabinet maker.

With Crutch Brothers came three employees: Colin Buckwell, the cabinet maker who is still with the business today; Eileen Lock, who had been their book-keeper and continued to do the same work for me until she retired some 10 years later; and Bill the upholsterer, who might be termed an old fashioned craftsman, eschewing any modern advances, such as stapling, but producing work to the highest standards. He always worried me with his mouth full of tacks, which he seemed to produce without any difficulty as and when required and could still go on talking! He could terrorise the cabinet makers by deciding to have a sweep up, creating a cloud of dust, just when they were polishing.

Sample curtain and carpet material was transferred to the back of no. 25, which we now owned and this side of the business was allowed to continue until Bill's death about 2 years later. By this time numbers 22 and 23 had been fully restored and turned into Tudor Cottage Antiques Centre which was ably run for us by Pam Young.

Cabinetmakers

The cabinet workshops were far too large for just one and thus a second cabinet maker was employed. George Chapman and Simon Nicholas, both fully experienced, came to us at different times. They were joined first by Martin Barth, who, in effect, was an apprentice and later Ness, who was to stay with us for 10 years until she set off on a world tour and found love in another country, after some interesting experiences. I always remember my first meeting with her at the workshops. She was accompanied by a large and very hairy dog that proceeded to roll on the floor and became completely covered in woodshavings and sawdust.

The last cabinet maker to join us in 1999 was Kevin Perry, who had spent much of his time working on early oak and walnut furniture for a local dealer whom I had known for many years. He has proved an invaluable and enthusiastic member of the team and is still with Derek Roberts Antiques today.

Clockmakers

The demise of Kent Clock Services, in 1983, and the acquisition of this property (no. 25), including a small building behind it, gave us our workshops for clockmaking where we employed Duncan Greig, Clive Collins, James Cavie and Damien McCabe. Clive was to become an invaluable member of the team. He initially started working for Brian Kuwertz when he still worked from home and transferred with him to Kent Clock Services when it opened and then joined Derek Roberts Antiques in 1983 when Kent Clock Services closed. Not only is he as a very fine clockmaker, but for some years has produced an excellent website for Derek Roberts Antiques and for the last two years has done all their photography.

Jim Cavie, who had worked for Kent Clock Services since its inception, transferred to us when they closed, but finally left to start up on his own account in 1991, as did Damien McCabe.

One other person was to transfer to us from Kent Clock Services: Duncan Greig. He had trained at Hackney Technical College and afterwards West Dean, where he met his wife Chris. He had a great enthusiasm for and knowledge of antiquarian horology which was to prove invaluable to the business. He, in effect, became the front man, carrying out all collections and deliveries, and the setting up of clocks in customer's homes and explaining their intricacies to them. Over the years, he became an expert on locating and resolving the various problems to which clocks are prone. He regularly travelled all over the country and even abroad, thus taking a great responsibility off my shoulders.

Unfortunately, his love of clocks could sometimes get him into trouble; I remember an incident when he had to deliver a clock up North. After setting the clock up in the customer's home, he thought he would make one or two other visits and finished up having dinner with a friend who had a similar interest in clocks. He phoned his wife to say he would be home a little late but when he finally arrived back well after midnight, he found himself locked out and I met up with him the next morning fast asleep in the car outside the shop.

One clockmaker who came to work for us for a comparatively short period was Mike Baker. He had been living in Rhodesia (now Zimbabwe) for many years and had built up a good clock collection; however, as things became increasingly difficult he decided to leave, but this was by no means easy as it was very difficult to get any money, or indeed anything of high value, out; however, his clocks were not thought to come into that category and he was allowed to drive out of the country with these; moreover, by melting most of the lead out of some of the brass cased weights, putting his wife's jewellery in and then sealing the weights with lead again and putting the brass cap on, he was able to take these out also.

He eventually left us and built up a good clientele of his own.

The Clerical Staff

With the exception of Rosemary Freeman, Eileen Lock, who came to us from Crutch Brothers, and Liz Stracey, who joined us in September 2000 and who, with Rosemary, has made an excellent team, most of the others were with us a relatively short while. One, I can remember, may have had a lot of sex appeal but lasted just two weeks. When I asked her to copy out a paragraph from a brochure she promptly cut it out and stuck it on a sheet of A4!

As we also took in outside clock restoration, there was obviously quite a considerable amount of paperwork involved with booking-in, estimates etc. We therefore needed someone very efficient to deal with this side of things for us. We were fortunate in finding a most capable lady, Pamela Pass, who was brilliant in keeping the workshop organised and the paperwork up-to-date. She ruled the boys in the workshop with a rod of iron and really kept them on their toes, woe be it to them if they did not fill in their worksheets properly! Pamela was greatly missed when she retired a few years later.

When Eileen Lock left we needed someone else to keep the accounts and by then were relying on the computer. Initially we used a book-keeper who worked from home and was apparently well qualified to do the work. It was only a year later when the accountants collected the books that we began to realise the problems, for instance there was around a quarter of a million pounds in a suspense account, all of which had to be allocated. After that we employed our own part-time book-keeper, Anne Woodward, who kept the accounts excellently; however, after a couple of years she had to leave for personal reasons and her place was taken by Pat McCombie, who proved to be the most efficient book-keeper we had ever employed. She was already taking care of the books for a large estate and a chain of pubs when we first approached her, but was still quite happy to take us on. Not only did she keep the books meticulously, year after year they came back from the accountant with no comments or corrections; she also did them remarkably rapidly and would also raise queries and make certain these were corrected even if it only involved a matter of pence.

Pat kept our books until we retired and this work has since been continued by Liz Stracey (who happens to be Clive Collins sister), who came to us from a bank.

Showroom Staff

So far as assistance in the showroom is concerned, we had only three people, Roger Lister, Leigh Extence and Robert Wren. The former had had his own business for several years, buying clocks and watches in this country and selling them to clients on the continent, mainly in Germany. We had done a considerable volume of business with him over the years and he had even sold Martin & Roberts wall regulators to customers of his in Germany.

As the years went by this business became more difficult, in part because of the recession, but also because of the declining price differential between Germany and the UK. He also had the misfortune to have a major theft which the insurance company refused to pay out on and indeed were only forced to settle some years later in an expensive court case.

Roger was of great benefit to the business, in part because of his contacts in Germany and his fluency in the language, but also because of his extensive knowledge of antique clocks. He was with us for some time prior to moving on to Christies, South Kensington, to take care of their watch sales.

We had known Leigh Extence's family for many years as they had an antique business in Exmouth where my sister and brother-in-law lived with their family. He had had an interest in clocks from a comparatively early age and when he was 19 went to work for someone who leased his own showroom inside Harrods. This was an interesting experience, giving

him a chance as it did to meet a wide cross section of society and handle some fine clocks, but when the lease expired the dramatic increase in rental made the business become unviable. It was at this stage that Leigh came to us. His work with us was mutually beneficial and he even represented us in America, but in due course, he decided to set up business in a small town close to his parents and other members of the family.

The last person to assist us on the sales side was Robert Wren who had an excellent background. He was first and foremost a great enthusiast, knew many people in the clock world and had his own business at the coast prior to selling up and doing a course at West Dean, where he acquitted himself very well. At the time he joined us he was working part-time at the British Museum, teaching at West Dean, and assisting at Christies, South Kensington, around the time of their clock and watch sales.

Initially he spent most of his time at the bench, but this was a misuse of his talents as his knowledge of and enthusiasm for horology, together with his ability to communicate this to clients meant that he was much better placed in the showroom helping customers. Since the business has been taken over by Paul Archard his work has advanced in this area. He now produces, in conjunction with Clive Collins, all the catalogues, attends fairs where they are exhibiting and makes overseas trips on behalf of the business.

Outworkers

Most crafts, and in particular clockmaking, have relied on outworkers to produce the end product. These may really be divided into two: those who are basically clockmakers but have specialised in producing various components of a clock, at which they become extremely proficient; examples would be hands, chains, fuses, chronometer detents and escapements. Those where other skills than clockmaking are primarily required would be dial makers, particularly those who produce or restore hard enamelled and painted dials, engravers, gilders and case makers.

We had one clock through our hands once which still had all the notes on its manufacture with it. Nine different craftsmen were involved.

Although today clock restorers have to be far more resourceful and able to make most of the components required themselves, they still need to use outworkers such as enamellers, painters, dial restorers, glass specialists, brass casters, engravers and cabinet makers. Moreover, some restorers specialise in different types of clock such as carriage clocks and chronometers, whereas others, for instance, become experts at putting back the repeat work or alarms on early clocks which demands considerable experience because of the different designs used at various times by individual makers.

In our own business, although we had considerable in-house skills, we still had to rely on the ability of many of the outworkers already mentioned and even, for instance, marble manufacturers if we needed a new base for a skeleton clock. On occasions, we even had to seek assistance abroad. Sadly nowadays the craftsmen who have such skills are becoming increasingly scarce. Institutions such as West Dean are invaluable in this respect in training graduates in many different crafts such as clock and cabinet-making, porcelain repair, musical instruments etc.

In addition, we sometimes put out complex restorations to people who had more experience than we did in the particular area required. An example of this is the clock by Cockey (Fig 41) which demanded much careful research even before anything was done. John Martin was particularly valuable in this respect and carried out several other complex restorations for us. Although the case was made in our own workshops, the complex lacquer decoration was carried out by Rosemarie and Arthur Toomes, who were very experienced in this field.

It is particularly difficult for craftsmen, especially those working on their own, to take on apprentices as they cannot afford to pay them much, especially in their early years when their input will be low and of necessity they will constantly be distracting the skilled worker from his job and thus reducing his income. Moreover, there is the added risk that when he or she is fully trained, they will leave and work for someone else or set up on their own account and thus the skilled craftsman will get no return for all the years he has given imparting the knowledge and skills required.

Chapter 12
Customers & Other Dealers

One of the pleasures of dealing in antiques and indeed collectables of most types is that you are dealing with people who have a genuine interest in and love of the items you are handling and selling, and will thus view and discuss them with enthusiasm and, especially in specific areas, have a great depth of knowledge on the subject. Thus a conversation ensues which will be both interesting and enjoyable for both parties. The result of this is that mutually beneficial personal relationships occur and quite a few of your customers will also become friends.

The closer a dealer can work with a customer who is keen to build up a collection the better. Ways in which he can assist are by letting them know if something comes in he feels they might like to add to their collection and give them first refusal on it. Once their collection reaches a certain stage, taking back some of the lesser pieces or duplications, for instance, in part exchange, will assist them.

He can also help the collector in various other ways, such as offering an overhaul and maintenance service, advising on a clock restoration or conservation and indeed the general taking care of the collection, and, if requested, advising on and bidding for items which come up for sale in auction. Valuations for insurance are another area where a dealer can help and, should something be stolen, assisting with the negotiations. In our experience, loss adjusters very rarely debate an insurance valuation made before the item is lost; however, the situation can sometimes be near impossible if this is not the case and there are no photographs or reliable descriptions giving such details as size, wood, decoration, escapement, age, originality, etc.

It is surprising how often people cannot tell you what wood the case is made of, give you details of the dial or even, for instance, if it strikes on a bell or gong, or how tall it is.

Once a collection has reached a certain stage and the client is enthusiastic you can suggest books he might like to read, museums to visit, lectures coming up and associations to join. You may also be able to guide him on what clocks (in our case) you feel it would be best to buy; however, here the collector often has definite ideas as to the direction in which he wishes to head.

While we would never guarantee to buy a clock back which we were selling, as we felt it was unrealistic; they might, for instance, wish to sell it in the middle of a major recession, when it would be difficult to dispose of and prices may never come back, or you may have three similar clocks in stock; however,

in practice, we did generally buy back clocks if, for a variety of reasons, they wished to sell it, or if this was not practical, sell it on their behalf. If this was the case, we would try and make a modest profit on it, but if it was a serious collector who had bought several clocks off us we would, if necessary, be happy to sell it at cost as a gesture of goodwill. Apart from anything else, there was always the chance that he would spend some of the money realised with you.

Another factor is that if you buy an item for a little less than you think it is worth and then sell it for a little more, then it is far easier to buy it back and resell it than if you had sold it for a high price in the first instance.

Should a customer wish to sell you back a clock for any reason shortly after they have bought it, then we would always accept it, even if, for instance, they thought it didn't suit their decor; however, in practice, it only happened a couple of times in 37 years. On quite a few occasions when we have offered to buy a clock back customers have changed their minds and decided they want to keep it.

Husbands and Wives

Serious clock collecting tends to appeal to men far more than women, although purchases of clocks for the home, such as single longcase or bracket clocks, and maybe carriage clocks, is usually very much a joint venture. In these instances, husband and wife generally have similar tastes and all goes smoothly; however, when it doesn't, it can be highly embarrassing for the dealer and he will be wise not to get involved in the controversy. More than once I have quietly retreated into the office and waited for the storm to pass. Usually, in the end, all is well.

One of the more amusing incidents concerning husbands and wives happened many years ago. The wife collected small occasional tables and the husband clocks. After maybe a couple of hours in the shop, the wife decided that she would like a pretty little inlaid table priced at £35. She mentioned it to her husband whose immediate response was "well my darling, if you want it you must have it" and asked me to write out an invoice, which I proceeded to do. When I was half way through he casually remarked "Oh and by the way, add on the Ellicott longcase clock, it really appeals to me." This was priced at £325, some ten times that of the table.

One other similar event concerned an eminent man in the city. He bought a fine longcase regulator off us and paid immediately, but when I tried to arrange a date for delivery, he just said that he would let me know. After three months, I phoned again but the response was the same, as it was also over a year later; however, he phoned me that year at the beginning of December and asked if it could be delivered and set up on the 22nd of that month. He explained that he had bought his wife a particularly fine horse which he was giving her on the 17th and so she would be in no position to object to the clock being delivered a few days later.

One of the more embarrassing moments was when someone, who was not known to me, brought in a clock for sale. I asked him if he had any idea what he wanted for it as quite often they have sought an opinion from an auction house or another dealer first. He said that he had no idea of its value and I, after examining it, said I could offer him £1,250 at which point he flew into a rage and became quite abusive, saying it must be worth at least £2,500. This was more than a little embarrassing as there were several other customers in the shop. I said that I thought my offer was a fair one and if he wanted more he should try elsewhere. I saw it sold in one of the London salesrooms some months later for £1,100, but did not buy it.

Another fascinating aspect of dealing in antiques is the customers you meet from a very wide cross-section of society. Once you got to know some of them they will discuss quite openly complex and confidential aspects of their businesses which they could not risk talking about to people who worked in the same area as themselves, and this, to me, being interested in what makes the world go round, I often found fascinating.

An example of this is a customer who made high grade plastic bottles for perfumes etc. He would buy his machinery in Italy and to a lesser extent Germany; however, he would analyse the production potential of each machine, decide which components he could improve on and then ask for a price for the machine without these, accepting that it would invalidate any guarantees. The result was that his machines would produce 20-30% more bottles in an hour than those made on the standard machines of his rivals giving him a strong competitive edge. Although the manufacturers asked to see round his factory, he steadfastly refused, nor would he accept royalties from them to allow them to incorporate his modifications; however, he was quite happy to show you round the factory and explain how he overcame various production difficulties.

An entirely different customer was a Mr Zinfani (not his real name). He came into the showrooms one morning, smartly dressed and spoke English extremely well, although with a slight European accent.

He had a profound knowledge of antiques and paintings, and also knew a lot about period property, on which he discoursed at some length. He mentioned several well known people in the trade including one or two I knew and then, after maybe an hour, went on to explain that he had been commissioned to furnish some six substantial country properties which were currently being restored and which he described in some detail. He was reserving certain items which he thought were particularly suitable and would purchase the rest from the dealers he had already dealt with as and when the buildings were completed.

He was particularly enthusiastic about three clocks; reserved them and then went on his way. As time went by, I began to get somewhat concerned, so remembering one of the dealers he had mentioned, phoned him. His experience was similar to mine, but he had had rather more reserved and for somewhat longer, and had also heard nothing. We both then made further phone calls and eventually tracked down very many other dealers who had had a similar experience, particularly in one town. Interestingly, one of them said that Mr Zinfani must be alright as he was buying the penthouse suite in one of the new developments on the Thames. We eventually tracked down this development and I phoned the agents. Yes, Mr Zinfani was indeed one of their customers and he had decided in the end not to buy one as it would be too small, but he bought two penthouse apartments and they were currently busy converting them into a single unit. I gently asked them if any money had been forthcoming so far, to which the answer was in the negative. I then explained the situation to him and he also became more than a little concerned.

The matter was followed up with some urgency, and it was soon revealed that Mr Zinfani, although having a profound knowledge and indeed a genuine interest in art, antiques and period property, was penniless, but had great delusions of grandeur. Nothing could be done and indeed the antique dealers had not actually lost any money, although this may not have been the case with the property developer. Nobody, so far as I am aware, heard any more of him.

A good friend of mine, for whom I had much respect, had been buying antiques for many years. He had a keen interest in clocks and indeed had a good collection, but also liked porcelain and furniture. His house, a large Victorian one, on three floors, was completely full of antiques. It had been impossible to get into the room on the left as you entered the house for some time, as a longcase clock had fallen across the door. The windows had bars on them and two independent alarm systems were in place.

The room to the right was full of furniture, longcase clocks, etc through which you could weave a passage. Moreover, more or less every drawer you opened was full of antiques, usually clocks or porcelain.

The large main living room on the first floor had tables along all the walls so that you had to sit in the centre and on each table was displayed anything up to six clocks, with literally none of them going. George's trouble was that whilst he loved buying things, he hated parting with them and virtually never sold anything; however, he did one day offer me a walnut longcase clock for £450 that he didn't like the appearance of. Unfortunately, it had been altered, but I knew what had happened to it as I had had a similar clock before in its original state and it was for this reason that I bought it and had the necessary cabinet work done, which cost about £100, and restored it to its original concept. I then sold it to a London dealer for £650 who advertised it in **Country Life** for £1,250.

My friend George saw this advert and immediately expressed to me his feelings quite strongly that a clock he had only received £450 for was now being sold for nearly three times that sum. I explained to him that the cabinet work had cost £100 and that dealers in the West End had to achieve high prices to cover their heavy expenses. In the end all was well and our friendship was not endangered, but he vowed at that time that it would be the last clock he ever sold.

I can recall two other incidents concerning George. Because he was a busy consultant, he would usually manage to find time to slip out to view any item in a sale he was interested in but not to attend to bid on it, and thus this task usually fell to his wife.

On one occasion there was a clock he was particularly interested in and thus although it was only estimated at £500-600 he told his wife to bid up to £1,000. That evening he came home full of excitement and asked to see his clock. When he was told he didn't get it because someone outbid him and when he heard that it was for only £50 more, could scarcely contain himself, explaining that he found it hard to believe that someone had lost him the clock for a mere £50. Husband and wife scarcely spoke to each other for the next three days! If one was feeling particularly mischievous, even years later, you could ask George what the clock was like that he nearly bought in Sotheby's. The reaction was always quite dramatic.

The other incident possibly worth mentioning is a porcelain clock he saw in a catalogue but did not have a chance to view and, as his wife was away, had to bid for himself. He got to the auction only a few minutes before his lot came up and was just in time to dash up to the saleroom and buy it.

He then cleared and paid for it and it was duly packed up for him. On the way home in the taxi he could not resist unpacking and examining it. On turning it upside down he realised that the bottom half of all four feet had been broken off and replaced with plaster, quite skilfully painted.

He immediately told the taxi to turn round and go back to the auction house where he deposited the clock and asked for his money back. They advised that they would speak to those involved who would be in touch with him.

A letter duly arrived informing him that it was his responsibility to examine any item before bidding on it and that so far as they were concerned it was his clock and they would be grateful if he would come and collect it. Some fairly acrimonious correspondence then ensued and in the end they offered to put it up for sale on his behalf without any charge. This was by no means acceptable and they then offered to sell it as a joint owner, and would then cover half the loss should it sell for a lower figure. This suggestion was also rejected and it was at this stage they threatened to bar him from their showrooms, which raised the disagreement to such new heights as threats of writing to newspapers and his MP. It was after this that he received a cheque for the full refund; however, even then he was far from pleased as when the clock was put up for sale again the old description was used with no mention of the plaster feet.

Nowadays, probably in large measure because of the buyers' premium and the obligations auctioneers thus have because of it, such an incident would not occur.

Delivering and Setting Up Clocks

Many of the smaller and more easily transportable clocks, such as carriage clocks, chronometers and most bracket clocks, could be taken away by the customer, but longcase clocks, regulators, and some of the wall clocks, needed careful handling and setting up in the customer's home and usually fixing to the wall.

In the early years of the business, I usually did this work myself and indeed enjoyed it. It was a pleasant conclusion to the deal to see the clock ticking away in its new home, where it almost invariably looked better than in the showroom and all the family admired it. An additional advantage was that if you set it up carefully and it had been thoroughly overhauled and restored beforehand, then little was likely to go wrong and you wouldn't be called out for any reason to correct a problem. An additional advantage was that you got to know the customer and his family a little better and, having seen the house, could advise them on anything else you got in they might like.

Over the years you learnt what spares and tools to take to overcome any problems; for instance I found an old button hook ideal for sorting out snarled up lines on a longcase clock; a box of clock pins was necessary in case any fell out (they shouldn't do) on a journey. Spare pendulum suspensions were also useful, together with a punch, to fit them as they were easily damaged and some wax with suitable cloths to give the case a final polish and get rid of any finger marks.

Most clock deliveries went without a hitch, but I do remember a couple where I got into difficulties:

The first was in our very early days when I was delivering a very pretty little spring driven longcase to a fifth floor flat in Highgate. I got the clock and my tools into the lift and pressed the 5th floor button. Unfortunately, the lift suddenly stopped on the 3rd floor with quite a jerk and at that moment there was a fairly loud noise from the clock followed by the sound of various components falling onto the floor.

I went up and down in the lift a few times and when I was sure that I had gathered up all the pieces, descended to the basement, unloaded the clock and then reassembled it and knocked in the securing pins, two of which had come out, securely. I then tested it, when all seemed to be fine, so I loaded it up again, proceeded to the 5th floor and apologised for being late. Fortunately all went well and they were delighted with it.

The second incident concerned the delivery of a fine late 17th century marquetry clock to Cornwall, a gift, if I remember correctly, to a retiring company director. I had completed maybe 100 miles when there was quite a loud bang from the back of the car as I went over a pothole and on stopping I was horrified to see that the base had come away from the trunk of the clock. After some 300 years the glue had just dried out completely. Luckily it was a clean break with no damage to the wood.

I drove into the next town and went to the ironmongers and purchased some quick setting glue and soft rope, and proceeded to a quiet place where I could park and glued and tied the clock together and then put it back in the car and padded it up, making certain that no stress would go on the glue joints, and resumed my journey to Cornwall, which at that time was a slow one, made even slower by my desire to avoid any holes in the road.

Just before arriving at the customer's home I carefully undid the ties and examined the clock. All seemed to be in order and I gave it a gentle wax to remove any finger marks. At the house I first went in and ascertained where the clock was to be put and screwed a batten to the wall there at a height which matched some existing holes in the backboard. I then carried the clock in very gently, screwed it to the batten, set it going, put the hood on and then advised that it should not be disturbed in any way for several days.

The customer was delighted with the clock and when I visited him again a year or so later, I was pleased to see that all was in order.

Chapter 13
Buying Clocks

It was a miserable, dull, damp late November morning with the rain coming down in a steady stream; the kind of day which always has a depressing effect, reminding me, as it does, of the long dark winter nights to come. It is not so much that I dislike winter, indeed I have many happy memories of the beautiful snow or frost covered winter scenery, it is the lack of light. By four o'clock in December you can no longer take a walk in the country or just do some gardening and even when the sun does shine, which is most rejuvenating, one only sees it for a few hours.

On the morning in question, I had opened up the showrooms, but thought it most unlikely that anyone would come in on such a day and was almost surprised when around mid-day the phone rang; it was a lady from Staines who had a grandfather clock for sale. I asked her to describe it but quickly resorted to questions as she obviously knew very little about clocks. How tall is it? "It must be 6½ - 7 ft as it is quite a lot taller than me." What wood is the case made of? "I don't know anything about wood but it looks very pretty." Has it got a brass or painted face? Brass.

It was at this stage that she volunteered the information that the clock had a very nice chime, which would indicate that the clock chimed the quarters on four or more bells or gongs. If it only sounds out the hours, the clock would just be described as a striking clock.

To try and make certain that the clock did indeed chime the quarters I asked the customer how many weights it had, the significance being that if the clock has only one weight, it will drive just the train of wheels and pinions that concern the going or time train of the clock and therefore will not strike, the only exception being the grandfather clock which goes for just one day between winding, when, because of the short duration, one weight has sufficient power to drive both the time and strike-work.

The vast majority of 8-day grandfather clocks have two weights one for the going or time train and one for the striking. A much rarer form of longcase clock, excluding those made in the 20th century, were those which were provided with three weights, one for the time, one for the hour strike and one to provide the power for the clock to chime the quarters.

From the answers I received, the clock seemed to be quite a desirable 8-day under 7ft tall, with a pretty case, a brass face and a chiming movement which was well worth going to see, so after confirming with my wife that she would be able to take care of things, I set sail for Staines. It was before the days of the M25 and was thus a long and tedious journey with the traffic being slowed down by the rain and thus it was the best part of 2½ hours before I pulled up outside the lady's house, having been guided there by a friendly local newsagent.

I walked into the lounge and after exchanging pleasantries asked where the clock was, to which she replied, to my surprise, that I had walked straight past it when I entered the hall, which I immediately returned to. There standing on one side was a very plain oak longcase clock which had had the best part of 10" chopped off its base to fit into a recess, thus reducing its value by maybe 40%. It did indeed have quite an attractive brass dial, but with only a single hand which nearly always indicates it is of just 30 hours duration and thus should have a single weight.

I then turned to the lady and asked her why she had described it as having three weights when it should clearly only have one. Her explanation was a simple one. They acquired the clock shortly after they were married and at that time it had just one weight, but after 14-15 years it stopped and refused to start again. To overcome the problem, rather than getting it serviced or even just oiling it in the right places, her husband added a second weight which persuaded the poor old clock to stagger on for another ten or more years, when it stopped once again and the process was repeated and the third weight added. This time it stopped after just a year or two and they then, possibly fortunately for the clock, gave up trying to keep it going. The damage done by forcing it to go when it was crying out for a little care and attention must have been considerable.

At this stage, I quietly explained that it wasn't quite the type of clock I was looking for and suggested she put it into a local auction where it would probably fetch, at that time, no more than £10.

With the rain still pouring down and the rush hour traffic starting to build up, I arrived home just in time for a very late supper. Had I asked the lady a few more questions, for instance, had it got winding holes in the dial, which would have told me it was an eight day clock and whether there were two or three, which would have indicated whether it was just striking or striking and chiming, I might have saved myself a wasted day. I could even have just asked her how many bells the clock had.

Disappointments, such as that day had been, are all too

common in the antiques world, particularly when you are a specialist in your field and try to handle only the best you can find. This does not necessarily indicate a high price, but a good and substantially original example of that particular type of clock. For instance, on French carriage clocks the escapement, which may be seen through the top glass, is frequently replaced with a modern one, either because the original would be difficult and time-consuming to restore, or to improve time-keeping. This is particularly important if the escapement is a specialised one such as those used by Paul Garnier. A customer of ours had recently had a good example of just such a clock overhauled through local jewellers who had taken the original escapement out some time prior to us being offered the clock. We explained that the value of the clock had been reduced by around £2,000-£2,500 and we wouldn't be interested in it as it was, and suggested she take it back to the person who overhauled it to see if the original escapement could be found and reinstalled. Initially she was told that the parts had been thrown away, but on indicating that she would be looking to them to cover the loss in value of the clock, they managed to locate them and we put them back; however, it was difficult to eliminate the modifications carried out to fit the new platform.

When a dealer, particularly one in a specialised field such as clocks, is offered an item he has to be particularly careful that it is a good example in substantially original condition, to safeguard both the customer's and his own reputation. He will be laying out his own money and if he makes a mistake will lose at least some of it, whereas if an auctioneer takes an item in for sale it costs him nothing, and if it fails to sell, he can return it.

There are many ways in which a dealer can make certain that the clock in question is an original one free from any major restoration. The best of these is probably to, when possible, buy back items he has sold in the past which is obviously easiest for businesses which have been established a long time. In our case, by the time we retired, we had been dealing for some 37 years and thus there were thousands of our clocks with customers, many of which were likely to come back on the market at any time. Obviously the longer the period of time since you have sold the clock the better as the greater the profit you can offer the customer. It will also come back onto the market 'fresh' and no one is likely to remember it, and therefore the appeal is increased.

To be successful in buying back items, particularly from overseas, it is important that you keep records, including the date when the clock was sold and the price paid. A full description should also have been done and photographs taken, for insurance reasons, which will enable you to assess the clock accurately, even if you cannot recall it to mind.

One of the more amusing repurchases concerned a firm of leading London art dealers. They received a letter in the 1980s from New York solicitors saying that they were act-ing on behalf of the family of a client who had recently died. They stated that they had had the picture which the London art dealer had sold to their client assessed by a local dealer who advised them that it was a fake.

They searched through their records over the previous twenty years and asked various members of staff if they recalled the picture, but to no avail, so they duly wrote to the solicitors saying they could not trace the picture and asked if they had a copy of the invoice or knew of the date when it was sold.

A few weeks later a copy of the original invoice was forwarded to them, which to their surprise, was dated 1937 and indeed on searching back that far through their records, they found full details of the sale. The picture was one which was well known to them and they had no doubts as to its authenticity. They then wrote back, affirming their confidence in the painting and adding, maybe a little tongue in cheek, that they would be only too pleased to refund the purchase price should the solicitors wish them to do so.

A few weeks later they received a reply requesting that the purchase price (paid around 50 years earlier and now only a fraction of its value) be refunded and that as soon as the money was received, the painting would be returned to them, and this is just what happened. It must have been the best buy that a firm of art dealers ever made.

One of the things which keeps antique dealers involved in the trade, sometimes long after other people have retired, is its unpredictability. Unexpected discoveries, of which we have been lucky enough to have had a few, are now rarely encountered but one never knows what might be offered to you when next the phone rings. Sadly nowadays they are seldom items you are interested in.

Two of the more unexpected incidents which occurred happened in our early days. In the first incident we were called by a lady whose husband had just died, to see a long-case clock in the south end of Tonbridge. It turned out to be a simple oak 30 hour longcase in need of much kindness which was worth at that time around £10. Fully restored and delivered it would fetch maybe £30.

The lady was happy with the price. I paid her and started to take the clock out to the car, first the hood, then the movement and pendulum, and lastly the single weight, which is all these clocks have; however, as I picked up the case the base felt unusually heavy and so I put it down, and felt in it, and to my surprise found a second weight, which I removed. Again, I picked it up but still the base felt heavy; again I put the case down and now found a third weight which I also removed prior to carrying the case out to the car; however, as I put it in something inside it moved. On checking I found it to be a wallet absolutely stuffed with money. I returned to the house and asked the lady if she had lost anything, which she emphatically denied. I then handed her the wallet, at which stage I expected her to be delighted; however, she flew into a violent rage muttering, "so that's where the old swine kept it." Evidently the extra weights had been put on top of the wallet to conceal it.

The cursing and swearing went on with no signs of abating and in the end I just left. Foolishly I had thought that I might get some thanks.

Matrimonial difficulties did occur in a few instances and one was particularly unfortunate in that I was taking John Martin, who had just entered the world of clockmaking, on a tour to introduce him to various clockmakers to see their workshops.

During the trip I arranged to see a bank manager, who was anxious to buy one of our clocks, but wanted us to take something of his in part payment. It was difficult in that some of the clocks did not interest me and he had bought others quite recently and at too high a price for me to be able to sell them again; however, after maybe an hour or more, we had found a clock which I could afford to take in part exchange and he was happy to part with.

It was at this stage that the wife arrived home, obviously drunk and started abusing John and me in the most violent way, yelling and screaming that she was not going to let us steal her clocks. The poor husband was completely overwhelmed and all he could do was watch as we left the scene, being pursued by his wife down the drive.

I had to quickly get John to a hostelry I knew in the district where, after a coq-au-vin and a bottle of claret, we had recovered much of our composure.

I felt very sorry for the bank manager, who was obviously horrified by the incident. He did phone up and apologise profusely after we returned home, but had not got the courage to try and take matters further.

There were, in the early days, quite a few dealers who might be described as 'characters'. One of the most unusual was Death (pronounced) De-Ath who used to drive around in an old Rolls Royce hearse in which a couple of bones (femurs) acted as grab handles. He had a variety of outfits and could appear in the markets dressed as anything from a vicar to a bishop with epaulettes on each shoulder in the form of miniature coffins.

I remember, in my early days, visiting a dealer who lived in quite a large Victorian house. When I asked him why the staircase had no banisters and wasn't that a little dangerous, he replied that he had taken them down as it made it easier to get the longcase clocks up the stairs.

There was one lady, Mary Bellis, whom we used to visit who was a leading expert on early oak furniture and was very knowledgeable on the period in which it was made. One day she kindly asked us if we would like to see her kitchen, which we gratefully accepted. It was equipped in much the same way as a 17th century kitchen would have been and on Valerie asking her if she cooked 17th century food she immediately replied in the affirmative, as if it was obvious.

Buying from Dealers

Another relatively safe method of buying is from another dealer who has a good knowledge of the type of antique you are interested in. He will normally give you his own accurate assessment of the item, just as you would if the tables were reversed.

A good example of the trust between leading dealers in our particular field occurred to me some ten years ago. Someone whom I had known a long time phoned and offered me a rare clock which I found particularly desirable and had some knowledge of. We agreed a price of £8,000 for it and I said I would pay him when I came his way to collect it in about 10 days time.

To my surprise, I received a phone call from him some 3-4 days later asking if I would sell him back the clock as a customer who had seen it previously now wanted to buy it. He could, of course, have sold the clock to the customer as he still had it and no invoice had been issued; however, he had still phoned me. I explained that I had someone who I was sure would pay me £9,500 for the clock once it was restored, but that as I hadn't mentioned it to them so far, would sell him back the clock for that sum. The deal was agreed and I sent him a cheque for £8,000 and he sent me one for £9,500, to keep the records straight.

The unpredictable nature of the antiques world can, of course, be one of its drawbacks but also one of the great pleasures of dealing. This can be illustrated by a few experiences.

In the first instance, when I got into work one day, I was told that it had been agreed that I should go that morning to see a lady whose husband had died and who wished to dispose of his clock collection, around 75 in all.

I duly arrived around 11 o'clock that morning and as I entered the front door was aware of a buzzing noise. I introduced myself to the lady of the house who took me through to the back to show me the clocks. On opening the door to the room, the buzzing sound increased dramatically and as I entered, I saw that there were shelves on all four walls and that each one was covered with relatively modern, mostly tin, but some plastic cased alarm clocks. Ever since her husband's death, some 6 weeks before, she had wound all of them up, maybe 70-80, every morning.

This was some 20-25 years ago when they were almost valueless although now some of the unusual ones, such as those made for children featuring cartoon characters, may well be becoming collectable. I had no choice but to say that although they were interesting, their value was low and that she or other members of her family might feel they would like to keep them. If not, they could possibly sell them in a local auction. Maybe today a boot sale might be the answer.

Another sad case was that of a lady whose husband had just died. He was a clock enthusiast and enjoyed restoring them and when he was told some two years earlier that his days were numbered, his wife started buying clocks to try and keep him happy and scoured all the local auctions; indeed she even mortgaged their home so that she could go on buying clocks for him. The sad result was that she bought very badly.

Unfortunately on the day we went down, I felt a migraine coming on. On the way there we tried to stop for a meal but without success and by the time we arrived I was feeling far from my best. It was a large Victorian house and virtually every room she had was crammed with clocks. Sadly, despite trying hard for a couple of hours, there was not one clock I could buy, for a myriad of reasons. All that we could find was a large dome suitable for one of our skeleton clocks.

Fortunately the story had a reasonably happy ending. Somewhat later an American auctioneer visited us. I gave him her name and address and he ended up buying around fifty clocks from her for his next sale.

In total contrast to the two cases already described, I received a phone call from America one day. The person knew of me but we had never done any business. He had bought a fine Tompion bracket clock in London 20-25 years earlier but quite soon after he got it home he had a burglary which somewhat un-nerved him and so he promptly deposited the Tompion in the bank, where it had lain ever since.

He said that he was sending the clock over to London where he had thought of selling it by auction; however, in case it was of interest to me he would send it to us in the first instance. If I then wanted to buy it at the price he quoted, I was welcome to do so but if not would I kindly take it into one of the London auction houses for him.

The clock was excellent and the price fair, so within a week I had acquired a fine Tompion which had not been on the market for 20-25 years. Probably the clincher was that the customer was paid immediately and at a figure he was happy with. I was to acquire one other Tompion from a private collection in the States and another from Canada. In one case, we had to go out and see it and then had to carry it back, and in the other instance we knew of the clock and had no qualms about it, so bought it unseen.

Fitting Longcase Clocks into Homes

One of the problems with longcase clocks is their height, which unfortunately often results in their being mutilated to enable them to be fitted into someone's home. At the mildest, it results in finials being left off. With those which have a pagoda top, such as the classic George III clocks of this type, the pagoda is quite often reduced or even removed whilst in other cases the base is shortened, sometimes just by removing the plinth, but in other instances cutting off quite a chunk of the base itself. Unfortunately, the reduction of either the top or bottom of a longcase clock nearly always spoils the proportions and seriously effects its value.

An amusing incident occurred when I was offered a walnut longcase which was described as standing over 8' 6" tall.

I went down to Ashford to see it and when I walked into the hall saw a walnut longcase, but only apparently 7' 6", the height of the hall. I mentioned to the owner that he had described it as 8' 6" and he did indeed confirm it was. He then explained that he had had it in his garage for several years as it was too tall for the house, but that some months ago, when his wife was out for the day, he had hired a road drill and cut a hole in the concrete floor of the hall about 15" deep which would accommodate most of the base of the clock. He had then lined the hole with a waterproof material and felt, and dropped the clock into it and cut the carpet around it, but evidently even then he was in some difficulty as he couldn't put the hood on because the top finial was too high; however, he overcame this by drilling a hole in the ceiling, removing the finial from the hood, pushing the spire of the finial up into the hole, putting the hood back on and then dropping the finial down into it, which caught me out when I tried to remove the hood to look at the movement.

In the end, we dismantled the clock, reassembled it in his garden, where it could be seen that the original base was all intact. It was a fine clock which we purchased.

By fitting the clock into the hall in the way he had rather than reducing its height by, for instance, cutting down the base, he had preserved the clock but had put his marriage in danger as his wife was furious when she came back in the evening he had done it and found the whole house completely covered in a thick layer of dust.

One other incident concerns a small and quite early oak longcase clock standing maybe 6' 8" high. A couple from Tenterden came in and fell in love with it, saying it was just perfect for the 17th century cottage they had just bought and despite the low ceilings they were sure it would fit in.

The following week I took the clock to their cottage and they asked me to set it up for them in the hall, but unfortunately it was just too tall to go there, so they then said they would have it in the dining room, but again it wouldn't fit and so finally we tried the lounge, but again without success. At that stage we sat down to discuss the matter and as I glanced around the room, I realised there was a distinct slope in the floor towards one corner and indeed on getting out the tape measure we found we had a entire extra 2" there, which meant that the clock would fit with a little to spare.

On putting the clock in position it was found that the existing holes in the backboard of the clock exactly corresponded with two holes in the wall. I felt that this could scarcely be a coincidence and so asked them who they had bought the cottage from. They turned out to be the people who had bought the clock into me and I had bought from them maybe three months ago. The clock had come back home!

Besides buying from other serious dealers, you can quite often also do so from dedicated collectors; however, a little care is needed here as you don't always know the depth of their knowledge.

When buying from private customers, particularly those who have little knowledge of clocks, it is always far more difficult and genuine mistakes are likely to be made, thus considerable care has to be taken, particularly if you are considering making the purchase without seeing the clock because it is a long way away. In these cases, the advent of digital cameras and emails has made life much easier. It takes very little time and money to run off 6-8 pictures, send them to someone and if they request further views, send these also.

Buying Overseas

If you are buying from overseas, then the problem of assessing a clock becomes even more acute and in practical terms it has to be of quite high value as the cost of travel, hotels etc has to be taken into account and absorbed in any profit you might make; however, sometimes you just have to get off your backside and move fast if you are to acquire some of the more worthwhile pieces.

A typical case was a very fine French lyre clock of around 1790 with a superbly executed jewel-enamelled dial by Coteau who was almost certainly the finest enameller of clock dials at that period and had perfected the technique of jewel-enamelling. I had always wanted to acquire just such a clock. Thus when I received a phone call one day from the owner, a collector/dealer in North America who had recently acquired it, I immediately booked a flight and asked him, as I was travelling a long way, to reserve the clock until I had a chance to examine it. The next day I arranged for the bank to remit the funds immediately if I informed them that I was going ahead with the deal. This was so that I could then hand carry the clock back to the UK with me on my return flight if all went well. On the Wednesday I was in the air.

The clock proved to be everything it professed to be; the deal was completed and I then had a pleasant couple of days sightseeing and visiting the local museum and being introduced to the various staff members, prior to flying home. Unfortunately, our flight was virtually the last one in and only a single customs officer was on duty who had little knowledge of the import of antiques, the result of which was that I had to persuade an experienced customs agent, at around 12-12.30 at night, to come over to London Airport to complete the paperwork. By the time I left, with the clock, the Airport was virtually empty. The customs officer had said at one stage that he would impound the clock and deal with the paperwork the next day, but I rejected this because of the clock's superb condition and extreme fragility; just one knock could ruin its originality and probably halve its value.

Buying at Auction

In the early days, buying at auction was a very straightforward affair. The seller was charged commission, usually 10%, by the auctioneer and the buyer paid the price he bid up to and no more. There was no buyer's premium and no VAT. A high percentage of the goods were bought by dealers who acquired them both for themselves for stock or on behalf of customers, for a modest commission, usually 5-10%, depending on value. For this they would examine items, in our case clocks, coming up for sale and give an opinion and, if they were successful in acquiring them, arrange for them to be overhauled and then set up in the client's home, where practical.

Today the major auction houses charge the seller around 10% + VAT + insurance, usually 1½%, plus the cost of illustrating the item in their catalogue which can be anything up to £500-£600 or more, depending on the size of the illustration. Thus the total cost to the seller, including VAT, is around 13%-15%. The charge to the buyer, up to £25,000, is generally 25% + 17½% VAT, ie nearly 30% overall and there is usually an additional 5% tax to pay if the item comes from outside the European Community. Thus, excluding import tax, the difference between the amount the buyer pays and the seller receives has risen from 10% when we started trading to over 40% today. The improvements, so far as the buyer is concerned, are that now that they charge the buyer a substantial amount, as well as the seller, they acknowledge that they have an obligation to him and so give condition reports on the originality of the items they are selling and also produce far better and more descriptive catalogues.

Such a margin makes it very difficult for a dealer to buy at auction, particularly bearing in mind that he still has to overhaul and guarantee the item if it is a clock, and then set it up in the customer's home.

Many dealers are pleased to trade on smaller margins than the auction houses, particularly if they are dealing with regular customers and are also happy to take items in on 'Sale or Return', when, because they are not involving their own capital, they can offer to trade on much smaller margins. The advantages to the dealer are that by taking things in on 'Sale or Return' he is increasing the range of items he can offer to the public. Another advantage is that if you sell an item for a customer, there is at least a chance that he will spend some of that money with you.

One benefit that a collector has when buying from a dealer is that he can usually do part exchanges with the aim of continuously improving the value and desirability of his collection. This, of course, is impossible with the auction houses. A benefit of selling to a dealer is that you receive the money immediately whereas, particularly with specialised sales, you can easily wait six months.

A plus of selling items through auction, particularly those of high value, is the enormous publicity they can give to the object through their catalogues and overseas advertising. The sheer size of some of them also gives the ability to deal with large collections, sometimes involving more money than the vast majority of dealers can find. They can also handle a whole range of artefacts at the same time, which is beyond the ability of most antique dealers.

A factor which many people enjoy at auctions is their competitive nature and the excitement of winning a hard fought bidding war, often on the assumption that if someone was prepared to pay just one bid less than you, then you must have bought the item at the right price; however, this is not necessarily true and I have seen many instances of this. One of the most amusing, if that is the right term, was at a local auction many years ago, which was always attended by a lady who liked to buy at least one piece and invariably went on bidding until she bought it.

In this instance, she had set her heart on a particular picture and finally acquired it for £450 against on estimate of £200. Shortly afterwards, a gentleman sitting behind her offered to carry the picture, which was quite heavy, out to the car for her, which she gladly accepted. Not only was he the person who had bid against her, he was also the owner! This could probably not happen now.

One of my own lucky escapes was also at a local auction. Two clocks were included in the sale, lot 14 which I was not interested in as it had been extensively altered and lot 15, which was a fine clock. Unfortunately an acquaintance kept on talking to me as the auction progressed and I suddenly realised it was what I thought was lot 15 coming up for sale. It was estimated at £200, but a newly established dealer ran me up on it and eventually I dropped out and he bought it for £850. It was only when the auctioneer announced that the next lot was no. 15 that I realised what a narrow escape I had, I had been bidding on lot 14, the clock I didn't want under any circumstances. I think the buyer thought that if it was worth £800 to Derek Roberts it must still be a good buy at £850.

There are many similar instances which I could recount, but one in particular I remember well; whether it was at Sotheby's or Christies I cannot now recall. An overseas friend of mine was interested in a particularly fine decorative clock which was estimated at £12,000-£14,000 and which I thought he had a good chance of buying as it was not the type of clock which appealed to English dealers and collectors. To my surprise, the bidding rapidly passed the estimate and quickly reached £20,000. At £28,000 I gave my friend a gentle knock and told him that he was bidding far beyond the clock's value but at that stage the bit was firmly between his teeth and he clearly had no intention of stopping. He finally gave up the struggle when the bidding reached £48,000. There was an amusing finale. The person who was bidding against him turned out to be buying it on behalf of a museum and was being paid a percentage on the price the clock finally sold for. He had a somewhat impish sense of humour and came over afterwards and thanked my friend for running him up to such a high figure, and thus increasing his commission.

He was a man for whom I had a great respect. He was Jewish and he and his mother, father and brother all had, during the war, been taken to one of Hitler's concentration camps; I forget which now. He and his brother were never to see their parents again, but he was interviewed by the Germans and asked if he had any skills which could be of use to them. He immediately responded that he could repair shoes, which may, or may not, have been true and managed to pass a test they gave him. This was to save his life and, I believe, also his brother whom he said could also do shoe repairs. Following his release, he continued to repair his own shoes for the rest of his life to constantly remind himself that this skill had saved him.

In due time he established his own successful auction house where he handled items he was particularly interested in, mainly clocks, watches and cars. I always found him scrupulously fair in all his dealings, but he was never one to miss a good deal and outmanoeuvred me on at least one occasion. A book on his life story would make interesting reading.

Chapter 14
Selling Clocks

To sell clocks, and indeed most antiques, you have to understand them and know exactly what you are offering; moreover it is highly desirable, unless you are dealing with serious collectors or dealers, to make certain that they are all fully restored and in good working order before you put them in the showroom. To put clocks on display which are not running or need restoration is scarcely encouraging to the customer; for instance, all he may see when he looks at the clock is a badly tarnished dial and he will not appreciate how much the appearance would be improved by, for example, resilvering. Further confidence is installed if, so far as practical, all the clocks are kept running and to time.

To use an analogy, few of us would buy a car from a dealer which has dented bodywork and couldn't be started, despite his insistence that the faults would be corrected prior to delivery.

You also have to talk to customers to try and assess the type of clock and price range they are interested in and you certainly must not assume that anything would be too expensive for them. It is surprising how often a customer will come in with the idea, for instance, of spending up to £5,000 but when they see something that really excites them, buy a clock for 3-4 times that amount.

A good example of this was the customer who came in one day when Greg Dallimore, who assisted us in the early days, was taking care of the shop. He was wearing a sports coat which had seen better days and the rest of his clothes, probably old friends, were rather tired. He looked around the showroom and after some time asked the price of a particularly fine Knibb longcase we had in stock, the most expensive item we had in at that time, to which Greg unfortunately replied "Oh it would be far too much money for you", which scarcely surprisingly offended him greatly, particularly probably because he was a very wealthy man. He immediately left the showroom and vowed that he would never return, and indeed spent a lot of money with a couple of other clock dealers over the next twelve months.

I subsequently found out who the man was and learnt something of his collection; however, despite my writing him a letter of apology, he never came into our showrooms again until the day he died.

Another side of the coin was a young Swiss man who came in one afternoon very casually dressed in trainers and shorts. He spent most of the afternoon with me whilst I talked to him about clocks in general and discussed in some detail those we had on display.

Three days later he reappeared in the showroom and said that he had decided to buy his clocks from us as we had taken so much time and trouble explaining them all to him whereas most of the other dealers he had visited had not taken him seriously and spent little time with him. In all he selected 8-9 good clocks to buy.

When it came to writing out the invoice, he asked me to make it out to 'Sisterprovide' and as I probably looked a little surprised he offered an explanation. He had been very successful in business and by his early 30s had no need to work any more; however, his sister had not fared so well and, because of this, he was setting her up in business, buying stock for the showroom she was opening, and selecting one specialist from each field to buy antiques from.

On another occasion, a clock collector whom we hadn't met before dropped in to see us on his way to catch the ferry to France. He had a very good knowledge of clocks and took details of some of those he was interested in, and went off on his week's holiday. Some 3-4 weeks later, as I had not heard anything from him, I wrote and asked if I could help or advise in any way, and enclosed photos etc of a few other clocks he had expressed an interest in. The result of this was that he bought around 8-9 clocks off us and over the following years purchased many more, including a Tompion, a Knibb and a Graham.

One day I was visiting him with a colleague when he asked to see the wall regulator we were offering him, hanging up on the wall above a safe which was covered by a thick cloth with the words embroidered on it 'Jesus Saves'. There was a nail already in the wall in the correct position and so we hung the clock on this and then, as we stood back to view the clock, the nail on the wall gave way and before we could do anything, the clock descended down the wall, only to become wrapped up in, and stopped by the cloth at the bottom, as it slid down between the safe and the wall. There was no damage to the clock at all, not even a scratch. Jesus did indeed save!

One last example of the importance of trying to help customers and supporting them in any way you can was the successful businessman who came in one afternoon. He had started collecting clocks quite recently and had already built up fine collections in other fields, including cars, music boxes and post cards of local interest.

We chatted about cars, in which I also had some interest and, of course, about clocks. I noted those which appealed to him and over the ensuing months as and when anything came in which I thought he might like, I let him know.

It was a little later that he expressed an interest in acquiring a period turret clock movement and installing it on the staircase leading up to his office, to act as a talking point. Although we never normally dealt in turret clocks, we managed to find a suitable movement, restored it and set it up for him, and indeed it did make an interesting feature.

When he moved home we transferred and set up his clocks for him and after he sold his business we moved the turret clock to a large garage he had. An external dial was fitted and the movement installed on the first floor where it was on permanent display; however, it was realised a little later that an internal dial would not only be useful but also a fine decorative feature. This was by no means easy, but in the end a design was evolved which, whilst difficult to install, not only looked good but functioned well.

The last feature to be placed on the building was a sundial, something we had not attempted before and which threw up several problems because of the position and angulation of the building, but in the end turned out well.

Projects such as this cannot be costed easily and almost invariably take much longer than estimated, but are all part of the 'give and take' of a good relationship with a customer, as is, for instance, advising them on items coming up for sale in auction which they might be interested in.

I have no accurate records to hand of the number of clocks we sold this customer over a 12-14 year period, but it was probably around 100-120, ranging from carriage clocks to some particularly fine and rare pieces.

An added bonus is that, although I have now largely retired, I still value and enjoy his friendship.

Chapter 15
Taxes, et cetera

VAT

When we started dealing, and indeed for the first six years, none of the above applied, but on the 10th April 1973 VAT was introduced at the standard rate of 10%. Such a level of tax would have put a great strain on antique dealers (and also those dealing in second-hand goods), and thus they were offered the alternative of the 'Special Scheme' whereby you only paid VAT on the difference between the buying and the selling price, which drastically reduced the tax which had to be paid; however, you were obliged to keep what was known as a thirteen column entry of every item bought and sold, including such information as the name and address of the seller, the date of the transaction, the price paid, the purchaser's name and address, the sale price, the margin between the cost (excluding repairs) and the sale price and the VAT due. In addition, you had to make and sign a declaration on every invoice as shown below, as did the buyer:

"Import Tax has not and will not be claimed by me in respect of the goods shown on this invoice."

"I declare that I am the purchaser of the goods at the price shown on this invoice."

As the introduction of VAT had obviously not of itself increased the value of antiques, the tax, in effect, reduced the price the dealer received when the item sold and thus his profit margin; however, far more serious was the dramatic increase in the bookwork involved, probably of the order of 200-300%. Before this, all we had to do was record our purchases, with a stocktake once a year, sales and expenses.

In 1974 the standard rate was reduced to 8% and a higher rate of 25% introduced for petrol, which was extended some 6 months later to include domestic appliances, pleasure, caravans, jewellery etc. The following year the higher rate was halved and on 18th June 1979 it was abolished and a new standard rate of 15% introduced, which was increased just under two years later to 17.5%, where, at the time of writing, it still remains.

An amusing incident I remember concerned a leading cabinet maker. He was so incensed by the idea of VAT that he had special black edged headed paper produced with, boldly typed across the bottom, 'Death of Freedom in England'. All his invoices for the next six months were dated 30th March 1973, the day before the tax came in.

This cabinet maker, who was in Kent, had an excellent workshop with a very fine stock of old timber and veneers and was at the top of his craft, having been involved in it all his life. One of his great pleasures was in taking on apprentices and training them to be cabinet makers, but, unfortunately, the unions moved in on him, making constant demands which, in the end, he found impossible to meet and so he dismissed all his apprentices, which was a great loss to all concerned. What the unions, and indeed many others, do not appreciate, is that training an apprentice absorbs much of the time of the skilled cabinet makers and prevents them doing profitable work for the business. It is only towards the end of their training that apprentices start to make a useful contribution. If they then leave at the end of their training, it means a net loss to the business. An acquaintance of mine recently estimated that it cost him £45,000 to train someone for 3 years and sadly, because they so often leave after this, has discontinued it.

To digress for a minute, two of the more amusing challenges to VAT were:

(a) The appeal by the owners of Blackpool Pleasure Beach when they sought to get 'The Big One rollercoaster' registered as a form of public transport and exempt from VAT. The VAT tribunal agreed, but this decision was overturned on appeal.
(b) In 1991 there was an appeal as to whether a Jaffa Cake was a biscuit (VAT rated) or a cake (VAT exempt). It was eventually ruled to be a cake.

Import Tax

This was one of the most misguided taxes to be introduced and is a 5% tax on any antiques imported into this country from outside the EEC. It had been tried out before in one or two countries and the inevitable result was a fall in antiques coming into the country for sale and obviously the same must happen in the UK and will inevitably lead to a decline in the country, which until recently has been in the forefront, of goods sent here for sale. If someone has a painting worth two million pounds it seems extremely unlikely that he will be willing to pay £100,000 VAT or more correctly called import tax, for the privilege of selling it here when he can dispose of it in New York, Switzerland, Hong Kong or Singapore, for instance, without having to pay anything. Undoubtedly when someone sees the symbol in an auction catalogue that import tax is payable it reduces his interest in this item.

The effect of import tax can, to some extent, be mitigated by opening an Import Guarantee Account, which delays paying the tax either for two years or until the goods are sold; 5% is then charged on the sale price. The disadvantages of this account are that considerably more bookwork is involved and that a bank guarantee has to be provided for the maximum amount of tax which is outstanding.

Capital Gains Tax

This was introduced in 1965 to bring into the realm of taxation anyone who makes a profit from the buying and selling of property and many other items such as paintings and antiques; however, mechanical devices such as cars and boats were excluded from the tax because of the cost of the maintenance and renewal required. From the taxation authorities point of view, the high cost of upkeep on these items, which would have to be included in the calculations, could well mean that a capital loss would be incurred which could then be offset against capital gains elsewhere.

When someone argued that antique clocks were 'mechanical devices' and thus exempt from capital gains, his arguments were rejected but he won his case on appeal and since then antique clocks have been exempt from capital gains tax, making them appreciably more attractive from an investment point of view than other antiques.

Inflation

Inflation was to be the downfall of many antique dealers. All too often they would consider the rise in the value of their stock at the end of their financial year as profit and accordingly spend it; however, if the value of your stock has risen by 10% but inflation is also running at 10%, then in real terms you have made nothing. It is important to increase the value of your stock each year, at least by the rate of inflation and indeed more than this if the business is to prosper. It is essential that a dealer maintains, at a minimum, or even increases the quality and range of goods he can offer the customers if the business is to remain viable, or hopefully progress.

Retail Price Index

The rise in the Retail Price Index (RPI) which is a means of measuring inflation, averaged 7.1% in 1972, but in 1973 it rose to 9.2%, within a further year had reached 10%, and by 1975 24.2% at which stage it was putting a serious strain on many businesses. This was because, in effect, the cost of stock, which a business had to carry, as expressed in pounds sterling, had to increase by 24.2% to carry the same quantity of stock, which then translated in the accounts of companies as a profit of 24.2%, that, in effect, had not been achieved but tax had to be paid on.

Stock Relief

To counteract this, and save many firms from bankruptcy, stock relief was introduced in which any increase in the value of the stock, up to the level of inflation, was allowable against the assessed profits of the company. This was invaluable to antique dealers as it enabled them to maintain their stock levels and thus their turnover without any tax liability.

It was at this stage that the country was forced to devalue; however, we were assured by Harold Wilson, somewhat optimistically, that this "would not affect the pound in our pocket."

By 1976, inflation had fallen to 16.5%, the following year 15.8% and by 1978 it had nearly halved, to 8.3%. By 1980 it had unfortunately risen again to 16%, but within two years it had dropped back to 8.6% and the following year 4.8%, but 1983 saw it fall to 4.6% and the only year since then when it gave concern was 1990 when it rose to 9.5%. Over the last 14 years it has never been higher than 3.5%.

Recession

There were three recessions, each different, during our business career:

1. **The early 1970s** – when the Gross Domestic Product fell by 3.1% between its peak in 1973 and its trough in 1975.
2. **The early 1980s** – with the GDP falling by 6.1% between its peak in 1979 and its trough some two years later.
3. **The early 1990s** – with the GDP falling by 2.5% between its peak in 1990 and its trough in 1991. This was the recession that was to lead to the crash in the property market and many people being dispossessed of their homes. We personally were in a difficult position at this time as we were engaged in buying not only another more expensive house, but also some business premises we needed which we had been trying to acquire for many years; however, thanks to the fact that we owned outright our existing business premises, some five properties in all and our home, we were not under nearly as much pressure as our colleagues in central London who had expensive rents or leases to maintain and high rates. It was this recession which was to see the demise of several of the leading West End dealers.

As with all recessions, although it brings difficulties, it also gives rise to opportunities because of falling prices and the pressure on people to sell. If you have capital at this stage you can buy advantageously and then, because of this, pass these items on to your customers, with a modest profit. It even paid to sell off existing stock at cost, or even some loss, to buy fresh stock at more favourable prices.

It is also surprising how, with a little effort and going round other dealers and talking to them, and finding out what their customers want and conversely seeing if they have anything you could buy from them for your clients, how much business you can generate. On one occasion I sold four clocks in a day by doing this.

Interest Rates

These are often associated with recessions and put a great strain on any business which has over-committed itself when times were good. The dramatic fluctuations in interest rates is a relatively new phenomenon and it is interesting to briefly trace their movements back over the centuries.

In 1696, the first recorded year, it was 6%, but the following year fell to half this and indeed over the next 150 years only fluctuated between 2½% and 5%, the one exception being 1839 when it again reached 6%. In October 1847 it peaked, for a brief period, at 8%, and this occurred again in December 1863. In September 1864 an all time high was briefly reached but by the following year it had dropped back to around 4%. These kind of fluctuations continued for the rest of the century with the average rate being about 4%, which was to continue until the outbreak of the First World War in 1914 when, for a very short period, it reached 10%. Thereafter it settled around 5-6% and this level of interest was to continue to fall right through until June 1932 by which time it had dropped to 2%. From then on it was to remain at this level until the nation recovered from the Great Recession, and the 2% rate then continued right through until the end of the Second World War and beyond. Thereafter until November 1967 it fluctuated between 2.5% and 6.00% with one or two exceptions, but thereafter there was an inexorable rise reaching 9% in December 1972, and 13% in November 1973. It was to remain at a high level for the next three years, peaking at 15% in October 1976, during which year it never dropped below 9%; however, even at these high levels, a good dealer, if he was turning his stock over 2-3 times a year and making say 20-25%, could afford to take the risk of borrowing money if he was well covered.

In 1977 the rates gradually fell back to 6-7% before rising the following year to 12½% and in 1979 to a new peak of 17% which meant that the average bank customer was paying over 20% for his borrowings. Thereafter they eased back over the next year to around 12-14%. Unfortunately, this was at the time of a recession and so dealers were being squeezed by both high interest rates on their borrowings and poor sales.

The years 1981-1984 continued at a relatively high interest rate, only dropping below 10% for the first time in October 1982. Thereafter they continued to fall quickly, going to 8.0% in March 1986. Sadly they then rose again after this fluctuation to between a high of 13.75% in January 1985 and a low of 8.375% in December 1987. A rate approaching this was maintained until the following July, by which time yet another recession was upon us, with the rate rising by October 1989 to nearly 15% prior to slowly dropping over the next two years to 6.87%. Since then the rate has continued to fall and has been under 5% for the last four years.

The Buyers Premium

The figures for this section were kindly supplied by Christies and will vary appreciably between the various auction houses.

When we started business in 1967 there was no buyers premium. The price you bid was the price you paid and the only charge levied by the auction house was a sum, usually 10%, paid by the seller. They were anxious not to increase this figure as it might well discourage people from selling at auction but needed to increase their margins and thus decided to introduce a charge to the buyer as well as the seller.

This, to many, seemed unethical as they were, in effect, saying that they were representing both buyer and seller, something which most people, including Solicitors and Estate Agents, are reluctant to do. Moreover, it is really a delusion as buyers will only pay (including the Buyers Premium) what they think the item is worth and thus the seller only gets the sum it sells for less the buyer's premium and the VAT on this in total 29.375% for amounts up to £25,000, the sellers premium usually 10% plus VAT, ie 11.75%, together with 1½% for insurance, and lastly, illustration charges, which, even for a single page, can come out at around £600. It is a little difficult to calculate the total charges, including VAT, which is non-refundable, but it is probably around 43.5% for items selling for less than £25,000, as opposed to 10% before the buyers premium and VAT were introduced. For items selling for more than £25,000 and less than £500,000, the excess of the hammer price is charged at 20% plus VAT. These figures are believed to be correct at the time of writing, but will inevitably change with time.

The following table shows the increase in Christies' buyers premium from Autumn 1975, when it was introduced, until 2005:

Autumn 1975   10%

January 1982 – July 1986   8%

From August 1986   10%

March 1st 1993   15% up to £30,000 ($50,000)
                              10% over £30,000 ($50,000)

March 31st 2000   17.5% up to £50,000 ($80,000)
                              10% over £50,000 ($80,000)

April 15th 2002   19.5% up to £70,000 ($100,000)
                              10% over £70,000 ($100,000)
(MKS, NYC, LA, HK, Amsterdam, Geneva, Zurich–Tel Aviv)
CSK   17.5% on first £50,000 and 10% over £50,000
Paris   17.5% on first €90,000 and 10% over €90,000
Australia 17.5% on all lots
Italy   18.5% on first €110,000 and 10% over €110,000

March 2003   19.5% up to £70,000 ($100,000)
               NYC & Geneva 12% above in KS

January 2nd 2005   20% up to £70,000 ($100,000)
                     12% over this in KS and NYC
          Paris 20% on first €110,000 (£70,000/$110,000)
          12% above this.
          Australia 19.5% to Au $200,000, 12% above this.
          Italy 24% up to €110,000 (£70,000/$100,000).

The abbreviations are:
KS = Christies, King St, London
AUD = Christies, Australia
HK = Christies, Hong Kong
NYC = Christies, New York
LA = Christies, Los Angeles

Since this table was devised, Christies buyers premium has been increased to 25% on sales from £25,000 - £500,000 and 12% of the excess of the hammer price above £500,000.

Chapter 16
Rare & Exceptional Clocks

From a comparatively early stage in the development of our business, we derived much pleasure from searching for, acquiring, researching and then restoring the more complex clocks. We were able to do this because of the fine team of craftsmen we had assembled around us, some working for the business and some freelance.

On a strictly commercial basis, this was not always a sensible thing to do as the hours of work involved in the research and then carrying out the restoration could be very high; moreover, because of their often highly individual nature they would not necessarily be easy to sell, being way outside the ambition of most collectors. On the plus side, they gave all who were involved in their restoration much pleasure and satisfaction, and the business the reputation both nationally and internationally of always handling rare pieces which you were unlikely to see in anyone else's showroom. It also meant that another fine and rare clock was conserved for posterity. Although in most instances those who visited us would not be interested in buying any of the rare clocks we had on display, they might well buy something else and in any case would mention the showroom to their friends.

Whereas clocks by Thomas Tompion, for instance, are highly sought after because of the fame of their maker and their superb quality, they are not particularly rare, several hundred still being in existence, and the vast majority, excluding his early examples and special commissions were made to a small number of standard designs; whereas the clock by Edward Cockey for instance, a very complex and rare one, was one of only four made, the second being for Queen Anne.

James Cox & Associates

We have always been interested in the work of this maker who assembled a fine team of clockmakers and other craftsmen around him to produce fascinating clocks, often of great complexity which were mainly sold to the Chinese market. How large the team of clockmakers was we do not know, but at one stage Cox petitioned the Clockmakers Company to employ forty craftsmen from Europe. This was granted, although the list of those who joined him was finally thirty two. It was a hazardous life, largely because of the fickleness of the Chinese market and the restrictions which were placed on importers. Most of the clocks were acquired to be passed on as gifts, usually to the senior members of the administration, including the Emperor and, of course, they were bought by the East India Company to give as instruments for trading rights. Cox was lucky in this respect as they allowed him to have what was called a factory which was in reality a trading station which was allowed to open for a limited period each year.

It was not so much the fact that these items were clocks as that they incorporated ornaments such as moving figures, fountains etc that made them highly prized. They were referred to as 'sing-songs' and had been coming into the country for at least 100 years before Cox and some other English makers appeared on the scene.

It was a hazardous trade because although there were good profits to be made, there were also unpredictable periods when the Chinese stopped buying, usually at the dictate of the Emperor, and if you had sent out a large number of clocks at one of these periods in the hope of selling them, then you were in serious difficulties as Cox found out to his cost on two occasions.

To overcome one of these problems, he sold a hundred items at Christies and followed it up with an amazing exhibition of twenty-three items, many of great complexity varying in height from 8 to 16 feet, few of which probably survived. This exhibition closed in 1772 but reopened the following year with 19 pieces which he decided to sell by lottery. The details of this are uncertain, but it is known that Thomas Weeks bought several items for his own museum, including the Silver Swan which is now in the Bowes Museum. As this apparently glides over the water, it lowers its head to catch and swallow fish, whilst being accompanied by music.

Cox's business continued until his death, believed to be around 1792. Those who would like to know more about this man are referred to Mystery, Novelty & Fantasy Clocks by Derek Roberts and various other publications

We have been lucky in having several of James Cox's and other similar makers clocks through our hands. One of the first surfaced in South Africa and may well have reached there in the first place via India.

Figure 38 a. **The clock by James Cox:** After restoration. (Opposite)

Figure 38 b. **The clock by James Cox:** Most of the components as they arrived from South Africa. (Above and previous)

We first heard of this clock (figures 38a & 38b) when we received a letter from South Africa, accompanied by a couple of photographs, asking if we would give them a price for restoring it. Evidently the story was that they had recently inherited it. Some twenty years earlier their father had taken it into a local clockmaker for overhaul. He had promptly dismantled it and put it in several boxes. Over the following six to seven years, the owner enquired as to the progress on the clock's restoration many times, but sadly nothing had been done and he eventually gave up and probably forgot all about it; however, after his death a member of his family remembered it and after visiting the clockmaker, who said that there was nothing he could do to assist, reclaimed it.

I replied to their letter explaining that we were far too busy to take on such a complex restoration for someone and that it would, in any event, be impossible to give an estimate without examining the clock in detail and that even then, the cost might fluctuate wildly; however, I did offer to buy it at what I considered was a fair price, given all the unknowns, and this was accepted. In the event, all turned out well. Relatively few pieces were missing and the clock, of outstanding quality, may be seen as it arrived and after restoration, in figures 38a and 38b. To restore a clock such as this gives much pleasure and also satisfaction in that it virtually guarantees its survival into the foreseeable future.

Another similar clock, but made by Henry Borrell, turned up, also in an unlikely way. I received a phone call from an American who dealt in furniture etc made after 1900. He said that a friend had bought the clock in a boot sale the day before, just because he liked the look of it. Although he said that he knew very little about antiques, he could recognise quality and this had it. He went on to suggest that he would let me have photos and that if I then gave him a fair idea of what it was worth, he would sell it to me, splitting the profit with his friend, and this indeed was what happened. I imagine their profit was in the 1,000s of percent. Sadly, I have never come across anything remotely similar in this country. The good thing about this transaction was that the clock was carefully restored and eventually reached someone who respected its fine quality and would take good care of it (figure 39).

Unfortunately, deals like the two just mentioned always have the potential to go wrong; however, as a dealer you have to assess the risks and occasionally take chances if you are to build up a reputation which attracts such pieces to you and inevitably, you hope, in these instances, to make a more substantial profit than usual.

Figure 39. An unusually small (overall height 15") and rare, late 18th century clock with automata by Henry Borrell. It was bought at a boot sale in America and subsequently acquired by us.

Figures 40 a, b. **This massive skeleton clock** was the result of the collaboration of five gifted men: Losada, who commissioned and sold it; John Moore & Son, the clockmakers; Nicole Frères, the most celebrated music box manufacturer; Colemann, the designer; and Stevens, the artist and sculptor. The author and his wife, Valerie, standing alongside, give some idea of its size. Three clocks were made in all: one for the Czar of Russia, the present example, and one other. (Above and right)

A good example of the type of clock we liked to handle was the superb musical and quarter chiming skeleton clock signed by Losada (figure 40); the result of the collaboration of five gifted men: Losada, who commissioned and retailed it; John Moore & Sons, the clockmakers; Nicole Frères, the most celebrated music box manufacturer; Colemann, the designer; and Stevens, the artist and sculptor. This clock, the result of their combined talents, must be one of the finest and most impressive produced in the 19th century.

The long duration movement, of truly massive proportions, has ½" thick plates and three very heavy chain fusees. A dead beat escapement and maintaining power are employed and the massive pendulum is most attractively decorated. The clock is enclosed by its own rectangular glazed case, again made regardless of expense, employing 1½" x ¾" brass for the frame and weighing some 80 lbs.

The Nicole Frères movement, circa 1847, No 5N15791, plays one of four operatic tunes at the hour or, at will, either Freischutz by Weber, La Fille du Regiment by Donizetti, Alessandro Stradella by Flotow and Don Pasquale by Donizetti.

Two other giant skeleton clocks by Moore are known. The first was sold to the Tsar of Russia and is now in the Hermitage Museum in St Petersburg, and the other one is in America.

Many of the rare clocks we restored were illustrated and thus documented for all to see in the catalogues we produced, of which one of the most interesting was Amazing Clocks, published in 1987. Clocks in this included the Radeloff Rolling Ball Clock (see figures 22a and 22b) with Cross Beat Escapement, circa 1660, which was previously owned, researched and restored by Professor Hans von Bertele. This was powered by agate balls running down a spiral track and as they did so pressing against a vertical bar, and thus driving the movement. The escapement fitted, which had been reinstated by Professor von Bertele, is known as the cross-beat which was invented by Jost Burgi. It uses a single escape wheel but two separate pallets, each carried by its own arbor but interlinked by two pinions so that as the clock 'beats' the decorative arms attached to the ends of the arbors cross and recross, a fascinating sight to watch.

Another very rare clock was a weight driven pillar or pedestal clock made by Joachim Oberkircher of Vienna, circa 1680 (see figures 25a and 25b). This had two main dials, one Astronomical and the other Astrological. The Astronomical dial has a rotating year calendar which shows on the outer two rings, the day of the month and the Saints days. Other rings indicate the month with the number of days in it; the signs of the zodiac show pictorially and also with their symbol; the hours of daylight, the times of sunrise and sunset, and the lunar calendar.

The Astrological dial was designed to tell you whether it was a good or bad day to conclude a deal or make a journey. It has hands which indicate mean and Astrological time. Seven rings towards the centre of the dial tell you the days of the week and their planetary deities in Latin. From this information the ruling one can be determined.

Other rare clocks in the exhibition included a month duration longcase clock by Delander indicating 'The Equation of Time', ie the difference between mean solar (our time) and the suns' time. A complex longcase clock by Charles Clay, a musical clock by Rayment in a Chinese Chippendale case similar to that illustrated in the Director and a very complex astronomical clock. There was also a triangular musical clock, possibly by James Cox, probably originally with automata; a seven tune pipe organ clock attributed to Jacquez Droz of Switzerland, a French world time clock and several others.

Mr Cockey's Masterpiece

The highlight of the exhibition, which epitomised the type of clock we strove to deal in, given the opportunity, was the complex and very large astronomical clock (figures 41a, 41b, 41c) by Edward Cockey standing some 139" high, of which just four are known. The first of these was almost certainly the one which Cockey sold to Lord Weymouth of Longleat, but despite being given full access to the Longleat records and spending much time researching them, we found no mention of it. However, some years later, David Pollard came upon a letter from John Ord, Lord Weymouth's Steward, to his master which reads as follows:

"Long Leate, December ye 9th 1706. My Lord, I have discoursed with Cockey about ye price of his clock and the very lowest I can bring him to is four score pounds and (he) vows if your Lordship will not please to have it at that rate he'll never part with it for less than 100 to anyone else."

Thus, although we do not know precisely when the Longleat clock was made, it was obviously prior to December 1706. Sadly, it is believed to have lost its original case in a fire later in the 18th century and is now housed in a relatively simple oak case.

David Pollard, in his excellently researched book on Edward Cockey and other Warminster Clockmakers, traces the family history back to 1601. Edward Cockey Junior first appears on the scene when he was baptised at the Parish Church of St Denys, Warminster, on 17th September 1669, which would be close to the date of his birth.

The Cockey's were a family of craftsmen, including pewterers, braziers, clock repairers and bell founders, and indeed this latter business, founded by Lewis Cockey, only died out in the 1950s. Interestingly, there are records of bills from Lewis Cockey in the books of the Parish Church of St Denys, Warminster, running from 1672 to 1697, mostly for work concerning the great bell of the church. The manuscript in Longleat House also records many bills from Lewis Cockey for brazing, repairing sawse panns, brasswork in the garden and keeping three clocks in order during 1701.

Edward Cockey, besides becoming a fine clockmaker, was

to take over the repair work at Longleat previously carried out by his uncle and also kept them supplied with many of the provisions they required, including wine.

Where and from whom Edward Cockey acquired his clockmaking skills is something of a mystery, as it is with many other famous makers, including Tompion, but undoubtedly his knowledge and skills must have been of a very high order to have been able to design and make the four astronomical clocks he produced. If he did not receive formal training, which seems somewhat unlikely, then he could have acquired the basic knowledge from his forbears and then built on this from pamphlets and books, and also from learned scientists, some of whom were known to visit the country giving lectures. In this respect he was probably somewhat similar to John Harrison of Longitude fame who started by acquiring his basic skills as a carpenter and joiner. Because of his deeply enquiring mind, Harrison was assisted in his education by a local clergyman who, amongst other things, lent him a manuscript copy of Sanderson's lecture on mechanics and physics which he copied in full, including the drawings. This is probably the start of his search for knowledge which, in over fifty years, enabled him to solve the problem of timekeeping at sea.

Edward Cockey's skill and knowledge in making the four massive astronomical clocks, entirely different from any other clocks made up until that time, cannot be doubted. The first, sold to Longleat, was a striking clock of month duration and had several signs of alteration during production which would indicate that this was the prototype and that Cockey was, to some extent, feeling his way at that stage. The other three clocks are all timepieces and non-striking, of three months duration, side winding and relatively free from alteration.

The Royal Clock

This is described in detail in MS 277 in the British Library entitled "Description of a very curious piece of clock-work made by Mr Cockey of Warminster. In his Majesty's Drawing Room at St James's." This piece of work, as I have been informed, was presented to Her Majesty Queen Anne, in the year 1705.

This clock undoubtedly stayed with the Royal Family until at least 1825 when B L Vulliamy, the Royal Clockmaker, carried out an inventory of the clocks and in Entry No: 163 states that "in the Ride" stands a "very old Astronomical month long clock in a japan'd wood case by "Cockey." In the remarks column he states "from St James's Palace". "Before the fire, it was placed in the Queen's drawing room, is a very curious clock, but not very commodious on account of its size." Memorandum. Lord Carrington has an exactly similar clock made by the same maker and these are the only two clocks of Cockey's making I ever saw. The name on Lord Carrington's clock is Edward Cockey, Warminster. Then added in 'Memorandum Nov 1, 1850.' "I never could discover what became of this clock."

We fortunately have one other clue to the identity of Queen Anne's clock which is from the Royal Pictorial Inventory. This is a watercolour illustration and shows an obvious Cockey Astronomical clock in an ornate lacquer case consisting of a large Corinthian column surmounted by a domed and inverted bell top caddy with further ornate cresting. Beside the illustration it states: "Removed from St James's Palace at the time of the fire. Made by Cockey. From Buckingham House originally."

There is little doubt that this clock still exists, but we will come back later to which one of the four known clocks it actually is.

The other three Cockey astronomical clocks, which still exist besides the clock at Longleat, are:

The National Maritime Museum clock

This has been, a little tentatively, traced back to Exeter in 1836, when it was restored by William Frost (of Exeter) for Lord Poltimore. It appears to have remained with Lord Poltimore until around 1920 when Mallett of Bath acquired it for £100 and subsequently sold it to Mayor Reginald Cooper who kept it until his death, after which it was sold by Sotheby's in their sale of 8th October 1965 when it was acquired by the National Maritime Museum for £2,500 and has remained with them ever since. This is the most original of Cockey's four astronomical clocks.

Lord Carrington's clock

This was referred to in Vulliamy's catalogue of the Royal Clocks.

The clock acquired by us

Which Clock was the one made for Queen Anne?

This was the question we had to try and answer before we proceeded with the restoration. We can immediately dismiss the Longleat clock as it has never moved from its original home, although it acquired a new case, probably in the second half of the 18th century. We can also dismiss the Carrington clock as this was referred to by Vulliamy when he was cataloguing the Royal clock.

The National Maritime Museum clock is a possible candidate but probably has to be excluded because the style of the case, which would appear to be completely original, does not match the watercolour of the Royal clock.

We are thus down to our own clock as, by default, the most likely to be the Royal clock, particularly as it is thought that the movement was separated from the case in the 1830s; however, this was not really strong enough evidence for us to assume for the purpose of the clock's restoration that it was the Royal clock and thus, when designing the case, we decided to copy the one in the National Maritime Museum, who gave us their very full co-operation.

The first stage was to make accurate working drawings of the case and then source suitable old stable timber. The details of the construction of the Museums' clock were noted by our cabinet maker, Colin Buckwell, and over the next 2-3 years the case constructed. The next stage was the lacquer decoration. In this respect we were most fortunate in having the services of Arthur and Rosemarie Toomes. Arthur's father had done a seven-year apprenticeship in Holland, the first year, interestingly, being spent learning to paint straight lines of any width or density. He did a considerable amount of work for the Victoria & Albert Museum and passed on his skills to his son and daughter-in-law. I met him a few times, but by the time of Mr Cockey's restoration, he had long since passed away, although he had left behind many pattern books.

Arthur and Rosemarie duly attended the National Maritime Museum and examined the Cockey clock in detail and found that some of the finish on different parts of the case was not that usually encountered but of a slightly rough nature to accentuate various aspects of the design and so they had to devise a suitable method of copying this. It was also decided that the details of the design on the case would be altered, as it was unlikely that two identical cases would be made and so the best part of a week was spent studying pattern books etc.

Some idea of the scale of the work may be given by the height of the clock, 139" in all. Indeed so as to be able to display the clock in our showroom, we had to make the upper part of the hood removable.

John Martin, a close colleague and friend, carried out most of the research on Cockey's Astronomical Clocks and our one in particular, and examined in detail the clocks at the National Maritime Museum and Longleat, and indeed at a later date overhauled the latter.

As a result of this, he realised that the following components had been changed: the seatboard, weight, pulley, backcock, pendulum, pulleys and escapement. In addition, the hands had been changed; the 'father time' figure and original sun were missing and the spandrels had been changed. The central hemispherical dome representing the earth was also missing.

A clever alteration, easily reversed, had been to reduce its duration from three to one month by moving an arbor and thus bypassing the first pinion.

It is not known with certainty when the alterations were carried out to the clock, but they appeared to be early to mid-Victorian. A curious feature was that the dial plate and chapter ring had been sawn in two at some time. The only tentative explanation we could come up with for this was to reduce the overall size of the movement and dial to a minimum, possibly for transport or storage.

The restoration of the movement, like that of the case, was of necessity a lengthy process if we were to get all the details right with frequent reference to photos etc, of both the National Maritime Museum and to a lesser extent the Longleat clock, and thus it was to be several more years before it could be put on display at our exhibition of 'Amazing Clocks'.

We were fortunate in that it was not to be too long before we found a customer in East Anglia who was keen to buy it and, probably just as important, had the right house in which to display it. Sadly some years later when he moved, he had to sell it because of the low ceilings in the new home. As this was in the middle of one of the recessions we had to battle through during our period of trading, we expected to have some difficulty in finding a new home for it, but to our surprise, the first person who was approached through an intermediary agreed to buy it and we even managed to give the owner a useful profit on the deal!

In strictly financial terms, it is doubtful if restorations such as this can be justified, but it gave all who were involved in the project great satisfaction, probably helped to raise the profile of the business and guaranteed that Mr Cockey's important masterpiece would be preserved for many years to come. It also meant that the clock could hold its head up high, even in the presence of royalty, as it had almost certainly done in the past.

For those who would like to know more about Edward Cockey and his clocks, we would suggest the following books:

Amazing Clocks – This was our own publication printed in 1987, which ran to 90 pages and contains John Martin's analysis and research into Cockey's clocks as well as a full description of it. It also contains details of many other rare clocks.

The Astronomical Clockmaker Edward Cockey & Other Warminster Horologists by David Pollard – This gives a detailed account of the Cockey family from 1600 onwards with a family tree of the American branch of the family. It also contains detailed descriptions of Cockey's four astronomical clocks from John Martin, Jonathan Betts of the National Maritime Museum and David Pollard who also deals with other Warminster makers.

Somerset Clockmakers by T K Bellchamber – This contains the first description of the Cockey Family and Edward Cockey's astronomical clocks.

Figures 41 a, b, c. **Mr Cockey's masterpiece,** probably made for Queen Anne, circa 1710. This clock dates from the first decade of the eighteenth century. It has a movement of three months duration with recoil escapement and one and a quarter second pendulum. The driving weight housed in the Corinthian column to the front of the case weighs 90 1bs, and the clock is wound through a contrate wheel driving onto a wheel mounted on the front of the barrel. Access to the winding square is through the left hand side of the hood.

The dial plate is 20" square and carries a twenty-four hour chapter ring. Within this is set a dish which rotates once in 24 hours. This dish is painted to represent the day and night skies and carries a cast gilt representation of the sun. The dish revolves behind a painted fixed shield which fully obscures the celestial scene between the hours of 8.15pm and 3.45am. Appearing from each end of this shield are blued steel shutters which rise and fall according to the season and ensure that the sun rises and sets at the correct time each day. The sunrise/sunset shutters are controlled through arms which ride on large cams which are each attached to one of two 9" diameter wheels with 365 teeth rotating once a year. Fitted to the bottom shield is a 10" diameter brass ring decorated with wheatear engraving which acts as a guide to the inner edges of the sunrise/sunset shutters. Within this fixed ring is a blued steel wavy edged ring which rotates with the celestial dish and attached to this is a cast gilt figure of Father Time. His hand indicates the hour, whilst the minutes are shown by the long gilt centre sweep hand.

Within the blue wavy ring are set three concentric silvered dial rings. The outer is a year calendar, the next represents the ecliptic divided into the 360° of the Zodiac, and, within that, is shown the 29½ days of one lunation.

The calendar and zodiac scales are fixed together and are read from the pierced gilt pointer fitted to the blue ring at 90° from Father Time. These two rings have been moved eleven days relative to each other during the eighteenth century to correct for the change, in 1752, to the Gregorian Calendar.

The age of the moon, read from the inner of the three rings, is indicated by the right foot of Father Time. Set within the lunar calendar, in a blued plate with gilt stars, is a moon ball and this rotates about a radial axis to show its phases.

In the centre of the dial, set on a silvered plate engraved to show clouds and rain, is a representation of the earth. It is interesting to note that, viewed from the earth, the sun and moon always maintain their correct relative positions in the Zodiac.

The design of the four large spandrel ornaments is unique to Cockey and is thought to represent the seated figure of Queen Anne.

The clock is housed in a reproduction case made by Colin Buckwell and decorated by Arthur and Rosemarie Toomes, which has been carefully copied from that of a similar clock by Cockey in the National Maritime Museum. (Above and next two pages)

CHR·PINCHBECK
LONDON

Figures 42 a, b. **Christopher Pinchbeck**. The dial and back plate of a complex astronomical clock giving the days of the week with their deity, the days of the month, the sign the moon is in, the suns place in the heavens, the southing of 23 stars, the age and phases of the moon and the time of high water in 30 ports. (Above and opposite page)

Figure 43. **The dial of a longcase clock by Joseph Finney of Liverpool.** The main dial displays seconds, minutes and hours, and has a year calendar which gives the fixed Festivals, whilst outside this is an adjustable ring for the moveable festivals. There is also a zodiacal calendar.

Around the inner edge of the dial arch is a half azimuth circle showing south in the vertical position and within this a rotating moon dial, engraved 1-29½ twice on the inner edge and with the 12 hours repeated every 90° on the outer edge. This, when read against the azimuth indication gives the moons southing. A blued steel hand, pivoted and locked at the centre of the arch, can be used to indicate the tide at any particular location.

In the centre of the arch is a complex disc engraved as a double celestial sphere. This rotates in the reverse direction to the lunar ring, keeping the moon's position in the zodiac correct and completing one half rotation in 18½ years. The setting of the moveable feast ring enables the date on which Easter occurs to be forecast.

Figure 44. **The dial of an astronomical longcase clock by John Benson of Whitehaven**, one of a small number of similar clocks made in Cumbria by local makers. Below the arch is a 9″ ring which intersects the chapter ring, marked and graduated Amplitude ortive 41°–E (0°) –41°S and within this the time (IIII – XII). The centre is engraved Meridies and the right side Amplitude Occa with the hours I – VIII and graduated in degrees. An inner ring is marked I – VI for daybreak and VI – X for twilight. On the left is engraved 20° - 0° - 20° to give the sun's declination north or south of the equator, whilst on the right are the ruling signs of the zodiac. The sun passes between these rings whilst below shutters rise and fall to give the time of sunrise and sunset. An aperture in the lower half of the dial indicates the state of the tides.

Figure 45. **An impressive green lacquer chiming and astronomical clock by Ellicott**, circa 1760, surmounted by a rotating globe moon. The dial indicates the days of the month, the months of the year, the days and months of the zodiac, the position of the sun in the ecliptic, the times of sunrise and sunset, the sun's declination north or south of the equator, the times of the equinox and the age of the moon.

Figure 46. **Thomas Budgen, Croydon**, circa 1740. The highly individual dial of a longcase by this interesting maker. The clock has a 24-hour (2 x 12) chapter ring with 12 noon being at the top and 12 midnight at the bottom, and inside this is a minute ring. A gilt hour hand carries the sun, representing its position in the ecliptic, whilst a steel hand carries a silver disc representing the moon. An aperture to the left of the dial reveals the days of the week, with their planetary signs, whilst the aperture on the right displays the months of the year with their zodiacal sign and the place of the sun in the zodiac. On either side of the dial are curved strips, each displaying the signs of the zodiac. A line from the centre of the dial passing through the corresponding point on the strips gives the time of sunrise and sunset.
In the arch is a rotating globe moon and below a circle of figures giving its age.

Figures 47 a, b. **William Robb of Montrose.** The history of this astronomical clock is complex, but it seems likely that it was made by him when he lived in Montrose and taken to Pennsylvania when he emigrated there, circa 1777-8, returning to Scotland circa 1780 when things got uncomfortable in America.

It bears a plaque 'Formerly the Property of the Nice Family', probably a corruption for the Neish's, who emigrated from Montrose to Pennsylvania in the 1770s. It was subsequently presented to the Historical Society of Pennsylvania by a Mrs O H P Conver and Mrs Anne N James in 1868. We repatriated it from America in the 1980s and sold it to the Royal Museum of Scotland.

The movement has an inverted train with the escape wheel at the bottom of the plate. The conventional lower part of the dial indicates hours and minutes and above it is the astronomical dial. A central solid arch represents the earth and its perimeter, the perceived horizon and behind this and the outer ring is depicted the sky by day. The moveable calendar ring carries an applied ring to represent the ecliptic and the whole ring rotates once a year.

In front of the ecliptic ring is a cursor with a pointer, which carries a representation of the sun, rotating every 24 hours. The sun has a pin on its reverse side which engages in a slot in the ecliptic ring, carrying it across the painted heavens during the day.

The cursor also carries two scales, one showing the sun's direction north or south of the celestial equator, and the other its altitude above the equator.

Many other readings can also be obtained, such as sunrise and sunset. (Right and opposite page)

Figure 48. **Guglielmo Meuron à Bologne.** A magnificent monumental Louis XVI pendule du Cheminée with grande sonnerie striking and incorporating a 20 pipe organ, height 37" (94 cm). The case bears close comparison to the work of Guiseppe Valadier (1762-1839), an eminent fonder and architect working in Rome.

Meuron's clocks and watches often bear the name of the town in which they were offered for sale, in this case Bologna (Italy), but spelt in the Swiss/French way, Bologne.

Figures 49 a, b. **Jacquet-Droz, Geneva.** This exceptionally fine maker very seldom signed his work, but there can be no doubt as to the attribution, his clocks being of highly individual design. The movement, with verge escapement, employs grande sonnerie striking on two bells and interestingly double six-hour strike, using a rack and snail with two sets of six notches in it.

The organ, with 9" wooden pin barrel, employs 18 pipes and two massive main-springs with chain fusees. (Above and next page)

Figure 50. **Robert Robin, Paris.** A full description of this superb clock, dated 1788, which shows both mean and solar time, and thus gives the Equation of Time, is beyond the scope of this book. Suffice it to say here that he was arguably France's finest clockmaker, producing this distinctive style of case, probably in conjunction with Thomire, which shows off so perfectly his superb movement with its remontoire. He was granted many titles, including watchmaker to the King, watchmaker to Monsieur (The King's Brother, the Counte d'Artois), watchmaker to the Duke of Chartres and appointed to the post of 'Queen's Watchmaker'. He was commissioned to make many important clocks including one for the King's Chamber, ascribed to hunting, 1.2 metres tall, for the massive sum of 30,000 pounds.

Figures 51 a, b. **World Time Clock**. A fascinating and probably unique world time clock believed to have been made in Paris in the 1860s. Sadly it was dropped some years ago and the case damaged. Using photographs of the clock we were able to restore it over a period of some 5 years. Unfortunately, shortly after it was completed the case (without movement) was stolen but a year later when we were reluctantly considering making a replacement, the police recovered it. There is quarter striking on two bells, unusual in that only one bell is sounded at the quarter, two at the half etc, with hour strike on a large bell. The going train incorporates a remontoire which lifts a small spherical weight which powers the escape wheel. As the weight descends the wheel driving the escape wheel pinion swings to the left and every five seconds a jewelled lever attached to it releases a fly which revolves one half turn, which is sufficient to allow the train to lift the weight to its original position. The escapement used is Graham dead beat with jewelled pallets. A single rod goes down from the movement to drive the fourteen subsidiary dials showing the time in various places around the world. (Left and above)

Figure 52. **The massive movement** of a rare weight-driven world time clock, circa 1880.

Figure 53. **Dents Shop-window Regulator, circa 1845,** believed to have been fitted with their own escapement, patent no. 8625, applied for on 10th September 1840. It is described and illustrated in full in 'English Precision Pendulum Clocks' by Derek Roberts, pages 170-171, published by Schiffer in 2003. ISBN 0-7643-1846-2.

Figure 54. **A remarkable pair of wall regulators**, of the highest quality, made by Charpentier in the workshops of Charles Oudin, a pupil of Breguet, it is believed for the 1862 Paris Exhibition.

At first sight these regulators appear to be identical; however, although the pendulums look the same, one is a compound pendulum made in three parts and beats seconds, whereas the other, although the same length, beats 80 to the minute. The latter has a duration of 100 days, whereas the other one goes for only eighteen. Both movements are extensively jewelled, even the pendulums being impulsed from one side by a jewel.

Figure 55. **One of many fine skeleton clocks** to have passed through our hands. Clocks such as this, where every component is on display, illustrates superbly the fine craftsmanship of the clockmaker who produced them and would take far longer for him to make than a conventional clock. They were often given as presentations, this one, for instance, bearing the inscription: "Presented to Joseph Norton Esquire on retiring from business. By his numerous work people as a testimony of their regard and esteem. May 1865"

Figures 56 a, b, c. **L Leroy & Cie Paris**. We have had numerous fine carriage clocks, both English and French and a few Viennese ones, pass through our hands over the years, including examples of the work of the finest makers, such as Breguet, Garnier, Courvoisier, Bourdin, Dent, Frodsham, Barwise, Jump, Kulberg, Barraud and Lund and many others.

One late but particularly fine maker was L Leroy et Cie Paris. He produced at least four clocks which might be described as masterpieces, probably around 1900. They were all 'humpback' clocks, a style first conceived by Breguet, virtually a century earlier. All of them had full perpetual calendar work, moon phases and grande sonnerie striking. The escapement, signed 'Echappement Special de L Le Roy et Cie', is a finely jewelled lever with helical hairspring which is superbly finished. A double index is provided which is linked to the micrometer regulation which gives the finest possible adjustment.

The clock has an alarm, the 12-hour dial for which is mounted on the backplate. Above this is a 24 hour disc indicating midday and midnight to enable the perpetual calendar to be set correctly.

The leather carrying case mimics the shape of the clock and allows its carrying handle to come through the top. (Above, opposite, and next page)

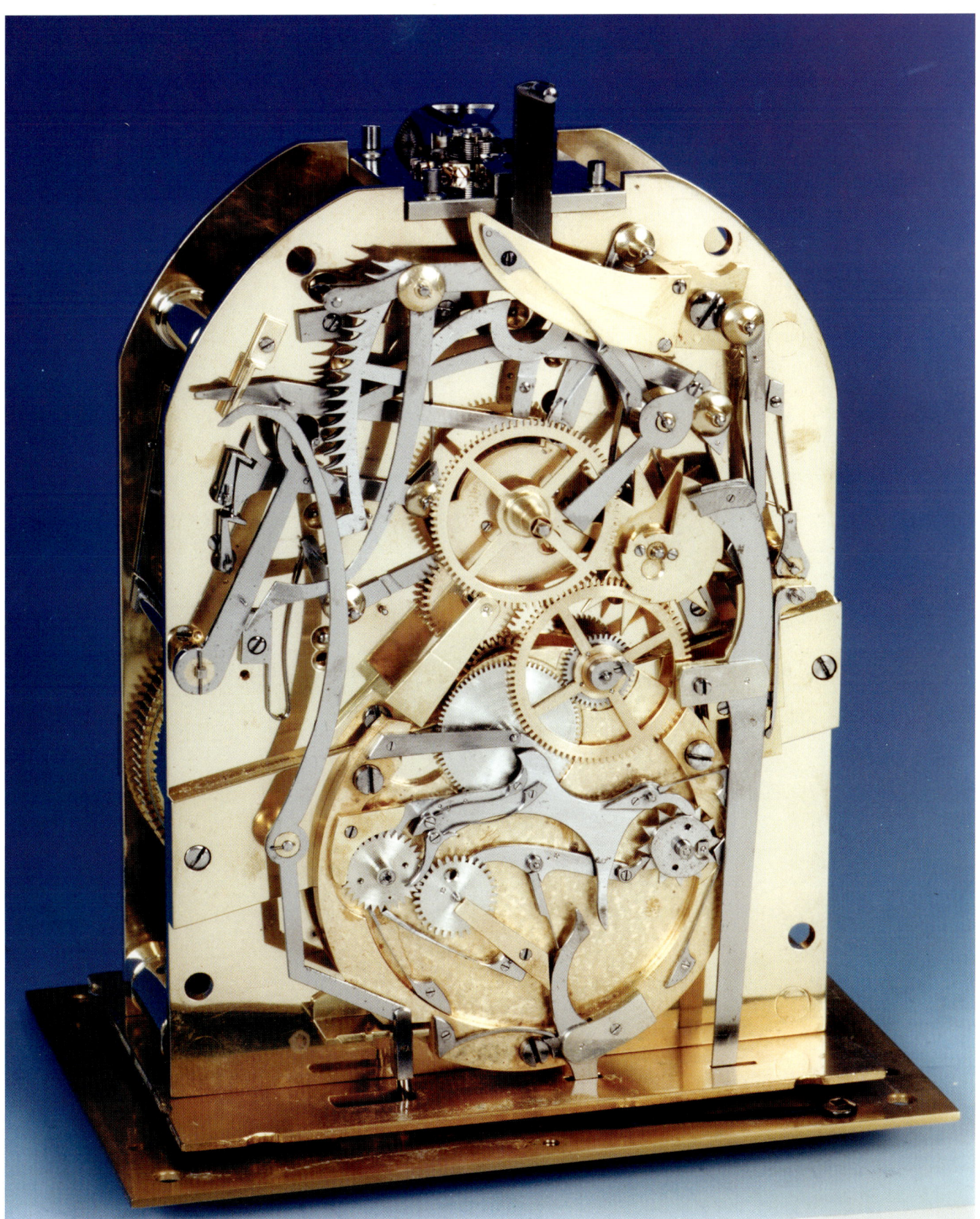

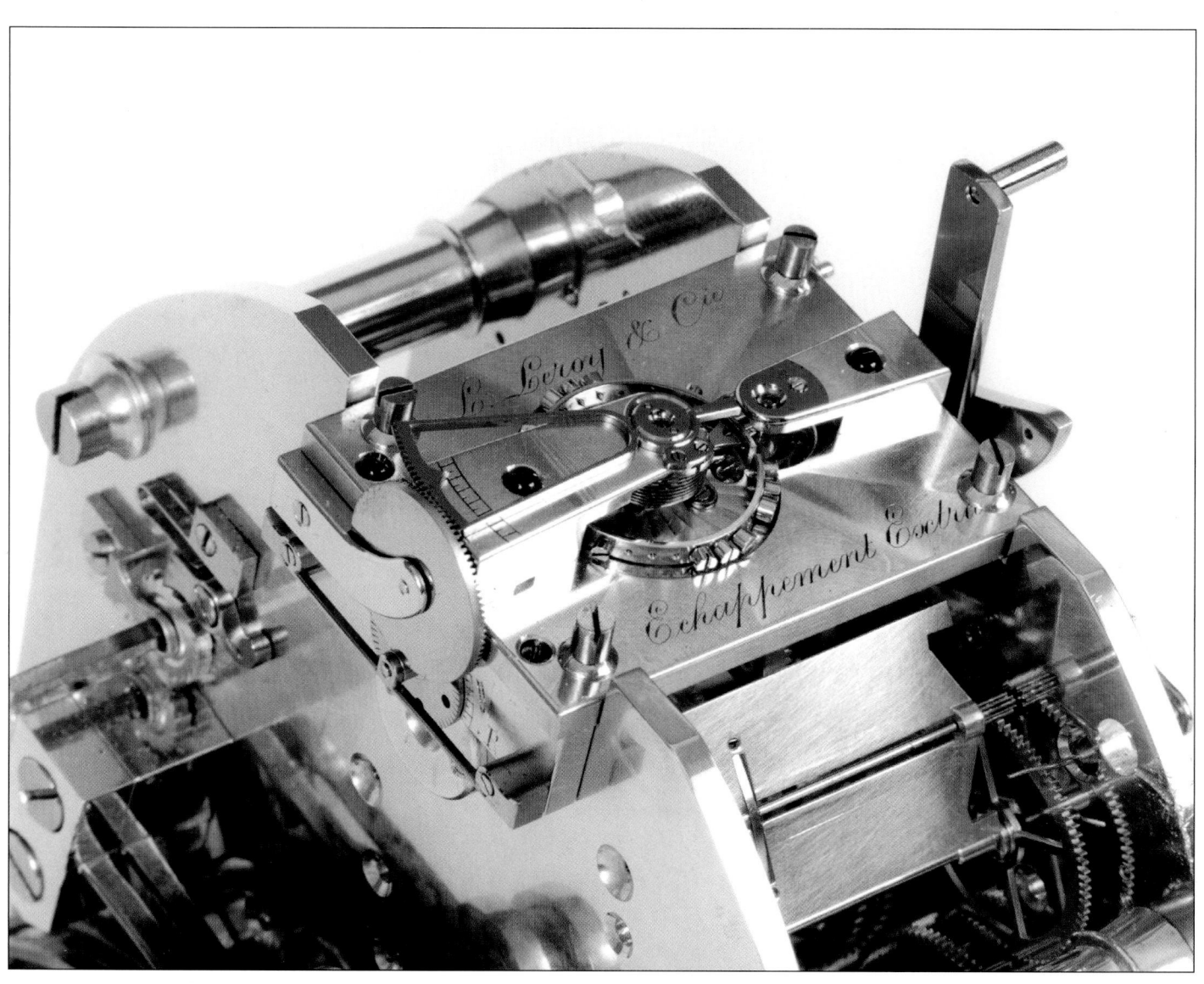

Figure 57. **Mr Caldwell's Masterpiece.** George Caldwell, the son of a clock designer, was born in 1872 and by the time he was 21 had opened his first shop. The clock was designed circa 1895-1900 and by 1920 he had virtually finished it, and it was put on display in his shop. By the 1930s it had travelled to Canada and went through various hands. We acquired it in April 1994 and repatriated and restored it.

The massive four train weight driving movement is beautifully finished with the components, estimated at 2,500, being numbered, and extensively skeletonised. It employs lantern pinions and a gravity escapement with mercurial pendulum. The hours are struck on a bell. It has hour striking, quarter chime and plays one of six tunes every three hours. It automatically switches to silent at night and, possibly a unique feature, sounds Kent Treble Bells every Sunday at 10.25am and 6.25pm to call people to church.

In the centre of the arch is a gilded strip which rises and falls with the tides. A disc, which is painted with clouds and has an aperture for the moon, rotates in 23 hours and 57 seconds so that it always rises and sets correctly. A tidal dial, which may be set to any port, is engraved with the state of the tides. Three apertures in the dial centre display a full perpetual calendar. A gilded centre sweep hand gives 'The Equation of Time.'

One of our principal interests has been precision time-keeping (Regulators) and we have had a very large number of these through our hands, including examples of the work of Graham, Shelton, Elliott, Arnold, Reid & Auld, Frodsham and Dent. We have also had regulators by many of the important French and German makers, the upshot of which has been that we have written three books on Precision Pendulum Clocks and thus are including the work of just two makers here, one English and the other German.

Figures 58 a, b. **Frodsham's House Regulator.** We were contacted one day by a leading jeweller in the Midlands whose extensive and beautifully fitted-out showrooms, with built-in cabinets, were being demolished to make way for a city centre development. The cabinets etc, had already been cleared and little remained but the Frodsham wall regulator seen here, and the furniture and fittings. Very little time remained and so a deal was struck and the regulator removed from the premises on that day. When they acquired the regulator from Frodsham is not known.

It employs Frodsham's own form of gravity escapement and a particularly refined form of mercurial pendulum with two long thin tubes to speed the response to changes in temperature. The lines from the two weights on either side feed onto a central barrel. The 24-hour dial, with subsidiaries for seconds and hours, is decorated with some of Frodsham's various awards. The whole of the outer case may be removed to gain access to the movement.

Riefler

We were fortunate enough to acquire two regulators by Riefler in time to include them in our June 1986 exhibition of Precision Pendulum Clocks, which was accompanied by a 125-page catalogue. One was a tank regulator made in 1904, which was retained by Riefler's for their own use. The second was a wall regulator, circa 1914, which was supplied to the Uccle Observatory in Brussels.

Riefler was probably the first clockmaker to apply a strictly scientific approach to regulator design and manufacture, and the results were outstanding. Their timekeeping was probably unparalleled until the Shortt Synchronome appeared on the scene and even after this Riefler supplied far more regulators, all tailored to meet the local conditions, than any other maker, up until the 1950s.

Figures 59 a,b. **Riefler Tank Regulator No. 78, built in 1904.** It is contained in an airtight glass tank and has a J1 nickel-steel (Invar) pendulum and Riefler's special escapement. Riefler guaranteed the accuracy of the thermal compensation of this pendulum to be 0.002 sec/day per degree C. (Below and right)

Figures 60 a, b. **Riefler Wall Regulator No. 341** with barometric compensation and electrical rewind believed to have been supplied to the Uccle Observatory in Brussels in 1910. This came complete with control panel and slave clocks. Note the mechanism for barometric compensation and the small weights to adjust the timekeeping. (Above and right)

Index

BLACK LION FARM
guest

BLFguest